Contents

A System of Opportunity

The 21st century has presented a number of challenges to those hoping to carve out a career in the political world. The rise of the internet, the expansion of the news cycle and the impact of socially led micro-movements have seemingly left nowhere for the ambitious politician to hide. For the politically active of the masses, the dreamer's dream was that we had finally entered an era of full accountability; every mistake or decision made by a person of high standing would now be open to scrutiny, allowing the voter to make a true and independently informed choice when selecting their leaders. This system, the intellectuals thought, would cut the wheat from the chaff, with those unqualified for office reining in their desires for fear of being found out, and those unsuited for the role would be ousted from their position and exiled from the political world by the masses.

Luckily for us, they were wrong.

The Changing Times

In times gone by, coercing the masses was an easy task for the pragmatic politician.

As a mouthpiece for central government and the elected representative of the masses, positions of power could be easily secured for a politician able to maintain a strong connection with their local community whilst cultivating a working relationship with the national media. The world, up until the rise of 24 hour news in 1980, was a much easier place for our political forerunners to navigate. The press operated at set intervals during the day, the morning newspapers would bring important stories to the masses as they ate breakfast and the evening news bulletin would update the public over dinner. With only two updates a day, it allowed politicians to present themselves to the masses as effective bureaucrats, freed from the pressure of constant scrutiny we could sit in our exclusionary boardrooms and decide the fate of the country without the media breaking down the door for the 'latest scoop', understanding their position as guests within the political realm, rather than its hosts. Challenges to this system came and went, problems that couldn't be solved quickly or that evolved beyond the point of repair would put our positions at risk, but only for brief periods before there would be a return to normality, and it wouldn't be until the rise of 24 hour news where the real problems would rear their head.

In order for 24 hour news to be a sustainable television product, the corporations that put it on the air needed to fund it by convincing companies to see the value of putting their brands and products into the advert breaks, which meant increasing viewership. To do this, it became imperative that the studios could not only pull viewers away from other, more exciting, television shows, but also keep the audience engaged with their product. This lead to an era of sensationalist news where reports would be based on a 'shock and awe' style of reporting, with journalists charging with the audience headfirst through an adrenaline fuelled day, jumping from one exciting story to the next, allowing the audience little chance for rest whilst giving away next to nothing in the way of details, bar a promise that the answers to everything were just the other side of the advert break. Unable to jolt the audience from one crazy story to the next continuously without causing a sense of confusion that would lead people to changing the channel, media outlets soon started inventing narratives to allow one headline to seamlessly blend in with another. Whether it be the crime rate, immigration or the latest big news scandal, stories were selected on their ability to fit in with the networks overarching story, whilst stories that fell outside the corporations strict boundaries were side-lined, regardless of their newsworthiness, for fear of alienating the fickle audience they themselves had created.

For the media, political narratives were the catch all they we're looking for. The masses had already picked sides in the ongoing ideological battles, so it became easy for the media to bend their reporting to attract a particular audience. Soon Politicians found themselves being reported in short hand, the gist of a statement being easier to fit into a corporation's news piece rather than a long winding quote. The constant sensationalism would soon reduce the audience's attention span far enough that eventually complete sentences would become too heavy for the viewer, with the media's reliance on narratives making it almost impossible for politicians to rehabilitate themselves to the masses once they were cast a bad guy in the first act of the news story. Reacting to this, audiences soon started to favour news outlets that designed their stories to pander to beliefs they already held, leading them to reject alternatives and believe they were the ones getting the actual truth, whilst others received nothing but propaganda from the enemy team. This would eventually lead to the split we see today with left-wing and right-wing media as the media started to pander to the audience they could sustain.

The developments of this era meant the Politician had a very thin line to tread. Our leverage over the media was depleted as they no longer required a sustained relationship with the political classes, all they required was quotes, snippets of information and characters to play the part in the stories they were selling to their audience. The 1980's and 90's saw many politicians being brought to heel, Jeffrey Archer, Michael Heseltine, Neil Hamilton and David Mellor were politicians of high standing brought down in the United Kingdom through media interference whilst in the United States, Reagan saw the exposure of the Iran-Contra affair, George H W. Bush saw his Treasurer sent to jail, and Bill Clinton found himself hounded by the media over his affair with Monica Lewinsky. Politicians simply became free real estate for a media who knew there was guaranteed money in selling stories which belittled them to which ever part of the masses had decided to perceive them as enemies. Yet despite having seen our power stripped away by the 24 hour news cycle, it wouldn't be long before Politicians started to adapt to this new world.

In the 1990's, the United Kingdom's Labour Party, under the leadership of Tony Blair, was the first to see the benefit in speaking the new language of the media, going so far as to hire Public Relations Guru Alistair Campbell, and flying out to meet Australian Businessman Rupert Murdoch, the owner of News Corp, in order to cultivate a working relationship with his UK media outlets. The Labour party soon started spinning their own narratives into the stories they gave the media, telling the story of a progressive party led my an up and coming leader, battling an unpopular and clumsy opponent in the Conservative Party who, wrongly, held the reins of power. Being given ready-made narratives was an attractive proposition for the media, who would save time and resources that would have been spent carrying out actual journalism, allowing them to instead print the stories as they were delivered. This cost saving was too good to pass up for the market driven news outlets, who even took to burying negative stories for fear of disrupting the narratives they had begun selling to the masses in order to maintain the capitalistic, yet positive, relationship based on the supply and demand of pro-Labour stories. The extra-marital affair of foreign secretary Robin Cook was soon supplanted by the decommissioning of a Royal Yacht, not something that would anger the parties working class support, despite the medias previously unrelenting attacks on the Conservative governments 'Back to Basics' campaign which was marred by the constant reporting of sex scandals and moral crises.

Up to this point, it would have been easy to write a guide on being a successful Politician. As long as Politicians held a monopoly over the dissemination of information, and continued to evoke a capitalistic relationship with the media, power could be easily maintained. Unfortunately however, this world would only last up until the 2nd Iraqi war.

The 2003 invasion of Iraq was not the first conflict to involve the Western powers since the end of the Cold War. It was, however, the first conflict where a reason for the intervention had to be designed from the ground up. The collapse of Yugoslavia encouraged intervention to halt the ethnic conflict, Haiti was invaded to put their democratically elected President back in power following a coup, Afghanistan harboured Osama Bin Laden and the Somalian conflict centred on the rebuilding of a failed state. The Iraqi situation, however, did not provide such a simple solution, despite the fact that the want for an invasion of Iraq had been part of American policy since 1998, following the signing of the 'Iraqi Liberation Act' after the countries dictator, Saddam Hussein, expelled weapons inspectors sent to ensure they weren't creating Weapons of Mass Destruction, a condition set after the First Gulf War. There was also not much interest on the part of the

American masses, or the wider world, to march back into a war against the belligerent state, regardless of the Dictators stance, or the economic benefits of conflict. This all changed with the 9/11 attacks on the United States, when the Bush administration, thought that the event could be used to put the appetite for war into the mouths of the masses.

The claim was once again made that the Iraq regime was developing nuclear weapons putting its regional neighbours at risk, as well as other NATO members, such as the UK, who, it was claimed, were as little as 45 minutes from attack. Politicians, along with their allies in the media, started discussing Iraqi links to the 9/11 attacks, with FBI director, Robert Mueller and Secretary of State Colin Powell, directly attributing Hussein's regimes to the attacks. Upon launching the invasion of Iraq, 57% of mainstream media viewers believed Iraq gave substantial support to Bin Laden's Al-Qaeda, 69% thought Hussein was himself involved in the 9/11 attacks and 22% thought Weapons of Mass Destruction had been already been found. However, as the invasion commenced it became clearer to the public that not only had they been lied to about Iraq's ties the 9/11 attack, but the supposed WMD's we're not going to be found outside of some aluminium tubes. As some of the media quickly changed allegiance to the anti-war contingent in order to shore up sales with the outraged masses, it was soon found that they had accepted doctored photos of alleged prisoner abuse, destroying their own credibility as the masses turned their attention to 'supporting the troops' rather than the war. For the first time both the political classes and the media were caught openly perpetuating a lie.

In previous eras, collusion between ourselves and the mass media would not have impacted our position as much as it would this time around. Previously, after each scandal it wouldn't be too long before the masses would be forced to return to us due to the monopoly of power we held over the political system. Each scandal would have its victims, a few unlucky politicians would be exiled from the party, some even imprisoned, and we would have to invent new philosophies to convince people we had changed, such as Neo-Conservatism, which expanded the aggressive rhetoric of the political right in order to match the rage of the post 9/11 masses who felt we'd been caught napping during the attacks. The masses would eventually return to their former political masters, once they felt the politicians, they had formerly seen as allies, had served a relative amount of penance and promised not to make the same mistake again. This would have the side effect of strengthening the Political Classes as the weaker politicians were purged and the masses doubled down on their previous allegiances, few giving up their emotional investment to follow a new political brand, allowing us new leeway in untested policies that may of struggled to get through in our previously reincarnations, such as the American Patriot Act, which greatly increased the monitoring of the public. Yet the system that kept the masses returning to us relied on the maintaining of the monopoly of power we held over people's political lives. The 2003 invasion of Iraq, however, coincided with the rise of the internet, and the public would soon be exposed to a new way of engaging with their political worlds, one that didn't include politicians.

In the same way that the printing press broke the grip the Catholic Church had on medieval society by cracking the monopoly it held on the Bible, the sudden equality of communication created through the internet and social media platforms such as Facebook and Twitter allowed for a new wave of grassroots socio-political news sources and movements to start quickly and cheaply. Without politicians at their centre, these New Social Movements (NSMs) abandoned policy-led agendas, and instead embarked on social crusades, concerned primarily with society, identity and culture, with wide eyed goals focused more on wishful thinking than thought out plans. They created new communities of people, many of whom might never meet yet will still strive together for the same goals, with social media aiding in the creation of a horizontal leadership model which allowed for many voices to be heard without them ever competing for the same spotlight. These social media platforms allowed the average member of the masses to involve themselves with movements for very little outlay, no longer walking door to door to canvas or post leaflets, they could simply share a post, adding to the 4.75 billion pieces of shared content Facebook sees a day.

As promised in Huxley's Brave New World, the public was soon bombarded with news from both the new media outlets and people on their friend lists, making it impossible for them to objectively break down each story and draw real conclusions. This avalanche of information meant that the masses soon started to lean more heavily on narratives in order to sort through the information, applying what they already believed to the stories they saw, and segregating good news from bad news based on whether or not it fitted in with their subjective world view; critical thinking was now, after years of struggling, a thing of the past. Soon the name of the news outlet reporting on the story, or the person sharing it, took on more significance than the news piece itself; If the Huffington Post presented a story, it was true, if Breitbart reported the same story, it was false, and for many, vice versa. This new media supplanted the traditional outlets with both the sheer amount of stories, as well as the amount of eyes on the product: in June 2018, the online Huffington Post saw 131 million site visits, Breitbart 64 million, with both outlets receiving more traffic through social media than CNN and Fox News, signalling the changing appetites of the technologically astute youth.

These new outlets were quick to react to the rise of the NSMs, and soon started adopting their beliefs into the own promoted narratives in order to attract them to their site, pleasing their advertisers and securing their income. Their reporting model allowed the leaders of the NSMs to offer commentary to a large audience with the same level of legitimacy as the site's journalists, blurring the lines between fact and opinion, further polarising their new audiences, who now split further from their perceived enemies as new battle lines were drawn between the demographics of age and location. The masses sought to exclude anyone with a differing opinion if it challenged their dearly held beliefs and regardless of any evidence, the wrong voice saying something was now enough to cast doubt on what was said. The new leaders of the NSMs were therefore able to carve out their own kingdoms in the national conversation, they replaced the politicians at the top of the political hierarchy for many by offering aggressive rhetoric to cover their knowledge gaps and an atmosphere of permanent revolution to build focus and unity within their newly built communities.

Canny politicians tried to unite themselves with some of these movements, particularly in identity politics, seeing the opportunity to rebuild an essence of block voting should they win the hearts and minds of the adherents, but these approaches have in large been rebuked. Their insistence in policy related goals is seen as dishonest gamesmanship, and the threat of their involvement in the cause delegitimises the cause for the NSMs themselves, their supporters seeing it as climbing into bed with the enemy. These new socio-political actors are aggressive, their supporters loyal and both remain autonomous enough to threaten the position of the political establishment. Luckily for us, within the democratic system there exists a defence that protects the political classes from this threat, delaying the inevitable reformation of the political sphere.

Once every four to five years the voter is picked out of their community, taken away from their political allies and put in a ballot box where they are told to pick what the next step in the county's social evolution looks like, and this is where we can control them.

The Modern Voter

In order to control the voter in the booth, we must first understand how they work in the world.

Political ideologues and sociologists are quick to develop incredible diagrams of society as they seek to balance how we are both a species driven by our own unique individual wants and desires, yet revel in the natural instinct to remain social beings, taking on wider responsibilities towards our various communities. Although these theories hold weight in certain fields, democracy is characterised by a unique event in the vote, where the individual is removed from their surroundings and placed in a booth where they are charged with making a hugely personal decision that will impact the lives of everyone around them. In this situation, when studying the masses their wants and desires takes a backseat to facets much easier to distinguish: behaviour and traits.

The ballot box offers an entirely different set of political circumstances to the individual than the socially active real world. In their day to day lives, people are free to partake in a wide range of activities and communities, covering a multitude of issues, thanks to the rise of the internet and the easy accessibility of online communities. However, when stepping into the voting booth they are then asked to choose from a range of politicians who have now been not only alienated from their regular political discourse, but also cast as untrustworthy characters by the voter's new allies within the New Social Movements (NSMs). When partaking in this democratic process, the masses are no longer being asked to select the policy or ideology they believe in, but instead which politician they believe will have a less negative impact on their day to day lives.

The rise of the NSMs disrupted the activities of weaker politicians who, outside the ballot box, started to see themselves being pulled from pillar to post to appease a support base who were happy to jump from one fashionable cause to the next. These politicians, although never truly accepted by those they sought to win over, have cultivated the opinion that the voter is a rational being who can be persuaded by both effective policy platforms and constant interaction with the political classes, with their involvement in NSMs simply being a rebellious stage of their political lives. They hope, and pray, that these changes to the wider world are temporary; the voter will remain rational and throw their support behind the politician who offers up the policies that are most likely to benefit them. These politicians therefore see political strategy as the cultivation of the best argument. They work to convince the masses that the manifestos they embody are the best option for improving the lot of the voters, and that they, therefore, deserve their vote. Green pressure groups would argue that it is rational to protect our environment, as we only have one planet; Marxist groups would fight for the control by the masses of the means of production, seeing minority ownership being the key cause of oppression; whilst liberals continue to put individual rights at the top of their manifesto, putting forward the notion that social restraints stem the progress of humanity.

These politicians will always go to great lengths to provide as much evidence as possible that their platform is the rational choice to the public, and each will be honest in their commitment to the cause. The rationality will though, in each case, be a straightforward exchange; by fixing subject 'A', you can expect a return of 'B', whether it be an exchange of money for social services or the sacrifice of oil for environmental longevity. Politicians on a weaker footing continue to be easy to spot, their rationality will always require a change to its environment in order for it to be effective. For example, the Republican party of the United States would argue that the free market is the key to opening up healthcare to the masses, but each election campaign includes some adjustment to free market healthcare policies to enable it to do so, the 'simple exchange' of goods now coming with a list of conditions to guarantee the sale.

Although the voter is a rational being, this style of argument doesn't work to draw them into the preferred choice anymore, and simply acts as a tool to legitimise the politician's own grievances with the world. The thinking of these politicians is to highlight what they perceive to be the most damaging aspect of contemporary society, and then lay out a plan which will lead to the eventual solving of said crisis. The issue with this, other than being a much centralised belief system, is that in today's environment whilst the voter is rational, they are not so in the sense that they will weigh up a long list of options and choose the one that would serve them best in the long run. The future is abstract and unknowable, and thanks to recent social changes, politicians are seen as corrupt and untrustworthy, so instead the voter acts with pure rationality, throwing their support behind whichever option will lead to the quickest, most guaranteed improvement to their life, seeking to remove the politicians as quickly as possible from the equation. This has led to the death of policy platforms, where a politician would back a series of reforms, each representing one interaction or exchange of information with the masses, in order to see a long term goal or objective carried out. Multiple interactions force the masses to ask themselves the question, 'do I trust the politician to follow through this time?', and as seen from the development of the masses attitudes towards the political classes and our allies in the traditional media, this is unlikely to return positive results for us if they have to ask themselves this same question continuously. We can still rely on issues which represent one overarching problem that we are seeking to solve, as they rely on only a singular question of trust, as do short term polices, which are economic in their reward. It's because of these changes, if an election is fought between a politician on the platform of environmental protection and an opponent who is simply promising to cut taxes, unless there are incredible circumstances in which environmental problems have a direct and quantifiable impact on the lives of the voter, the tax cut will always take the victory.

Economic rewards work well as cash is a controllable asset which is relatable to the masses, the more money you have, the better quality of life you can lead. Policies on environmentalism, like many based on social welfare, are not fully understandable to the average person, requiring a certain amount of dedication to study not generally found in the post-internet world outside of interested parties. This isn't to say in times previous that the masses were any more likely to put the effort into learning specific policy platforms, but the eternal oversight of the ideologies they subscribed to (mainly liberalism or Marxism) would at least predisposition them to the correct answers (dependant on what we needed). In the modern world, however, ideology is no longer a part of the masses political lives, but the individual will still need many social or wide reaching policies to be translated by a third party for it to be understandable within their own personal narratives. It was the political classes that originally held this role, translating policies along the ideological lines, but with the collapse in trust impacting our position, the masses now prefer working with NSMs to pressure politicians into desired behaviours rather than interact with them directly, either through protest, as seen with the Occupy Wall Street Movement, or shaming, such as Black Lives Matter. Because of this, there is nothing to convince the voter that long-term policy planning will lead to the desired outcome for the masses if they were to throw their support behind the political classes, therefore the rational choice is to vote, and support, the short-term gain (e.g. the tax cut) where improvement is guaranteed, and the politician needs to only be trusted with one exchange.

Each policy platform can, therefore, be one-upped with simple ease by a politician who truly understands what drives the voter to make certain choices. We need to move into a post-policy world where we offer the voters short term gains in return for supporting us, distancing ourselves from long term plans where we are asking the voter to trust us over an extended period of time.

Still, however, the poor politician will persist. Seeing the voter as a moral battleground, the losing politician tends to see their failures as an outcome of their opponent's corruption rather than the failure of their own plans. They tend not to improve their message or explain the benefits thoroughly enough to convince them to change their voting habits, instead they break down into insulting those that disagree, as we saw with 'deplorable' Trump voters or 'stupid' Brexit voters. Seeing each vote against their belief system as a personal insult, as opposed to a failure on their own part to understand the voter, this is an unhelpful attitude that weaker politicians took, which further distanced ourselves from the masses, as punishment for them simply acting in the manner in which they have been trained, and all for the sake of score settling through insult. The infamous 'swing to the right', they will argue, is proof that their concepts are on sound footing right up the moment their opponent sweeps in with a cash bribe to win support, whereas in actual fact its due to the weakness of their own campaign, and their arrogance of believing that the voter can only make right or wrong decisions, as opposed to honest ones.

The situation we find ourselves in is one of our own making. The seismic shift of the political environment, due to the rise of the internet and our cultivating of NSMs through our own mistakes, have changed the way the masses interact with ourselves, and we can't expect another shift to occur in order to correct the balance, as useful as that would be. Throughout the changes the voter has remained rational, the difference being that today's rationalities lead the masses to different conclusions than the ones of the past, as they remain guided by entities outside of our control. They interact very differently with their political landscapes, but this doesn't mean they are unmanageable, in fact, the break down in trust, mixed with the monopoly we hold on the political systems makes them easier to coerce, should we put pressure in the right places. We no longer have to manage the masses in their day to day lives, as they have plenty of volunteers for that, all we have to do is simply seduce them in the ballot box.

That said, showing up on Election Day and offering people a huge tax cut will not be enough to earn you their support, and even if it does, it will certainly hamstring your ability to govern well, should that be your intention. The cost-benefit analysis of the rational masses moves beyond the simple offering of people a cash advantage, it requires the voter to determine whether one choice offers a better return on the outlay required from them and the trust required from the other party. Tax cuts work within more sheltered, well-off societies, but you need to be aware of the wider world which will be vying for the voters' attention. The news is full of terrifying stories, the threat of terrorism, the imminent ecological collapse, the next super disease, and each of these can shift the voters' attention enough that the solving of that crisis is the one that will lead to election victory. It therefore becomes important to develop a frame for your election campaign that puts you at the centre of the problem as the only person capable of solving it.

Framing an Election

Although the masses now engage with their political worlds throughout the calendar year thanks to the accessibility of the internet, their attitudes towards the political classes mean that your first step into the political arena, outside of fleeting engagements, won't truly occur until the run-up to an election. Don't worry about being on the outside of the political debate throughout most of the electoral cycle: the masses will be glad for your absence, seeing any interaction with you being another step toward your inevitable betrayal. Your entrance into the political foyer will be signalled by the media awakening from its political slumber and scrapping together narratives from the NSMs to offer as their next sales pitch to the masses. You will see them, along with your political enemies, start to form loose, temporary alliances which seek to challenge your political credentials in order to delegitimise you in the eyes of the public.

The politicians you will face during this period will hold differing ideologies and ideals to you, and as time draws closer to the election, you are going to want to convince the masses to cast these politicians aside, along with their ideas, and embrace you and yours. Unlike other areas of life, Democracy, from the Politician's point of view at least, should be seen as a game of pure conflict. With a 'winner take all' outcome to any vote, there is little incentive for us to chase allies or draw up alliances amongst our peers as, at one point, there needs to be a winner and we don't want to risk supporting another in their attainment of it. Any relationship at this level would essentially work in the same manner as the *'Prisoners Dilemma'* with the advantage going toward whoever timed their betrayal better, allowing them to reap the benefits of the alliance (such as building a better relationship with their opponents supporters) whilst cutting the legs away of a future enemy. A prime example of this can be seen in the United Kingdom's 2010 Coalition Government between the Conservatives and Liberals, although successful in some respects, when the next election approached the Tory party quickly distanced themselves from the Liberals, arguing that whereas all the success could be tied to them being part of the coalition, all the failures were due to the restraints put on them by their partners in Government. At the next election, the Conservatives won a majority, and the Liberals returned their worst result since 1988, holding just 8 of their 57 seats.

The first few weeks of any election campaign will see the destruction of many political careers and most of these politicians will never be heard from again, so it's important you don't fall into any of the common traps that will haunt the amateurs, all whilst keeping your own campaign clear and concise. In order to achieve this, you need to promote a frame for the election.

A frame is an overarching topic that seeks to take precedence over anything else that may be discussed during the election; it could be immigration, environmentalism, social welfare or any manner of topics that are relatable enough that they can find a home in the psyche of the masses. Each politician you face will be leading their campaign with a frame that suits them, if they have a military or policing background they will generally pick security, if they come from the financial industry they will want to lead with the economy, and so forth. The trick is to find the frame that suits you and your experience, and allows for the highlighting of your strengths in dealing with the topic, whilst exposing your opponent's weaknesses.

During the 2016 Republican nominations, each nominee argued for a frame that suited them. Marco Rubio with his links to the Tea Party and Latino heritage fought primarily for immigration reform, Chris Christie with his firebrand rhetoric fought as a political outsider who could get things done, whilst Jeb Bush and Ted Cruz, as Republican darlings, fought as centrist figures who could appeal to 'Middle America'. Trump entered the race using his renown as a business deal maker to cast himself as the saviour of the American worker, with Ben Carson following, using his lack of political experience to argue he was untarnished by the so-called Washington DC 'swamp'. The Republican voters were therefore given a choice of voting on political reform, immigration, the American worker or the Republican philosophy, each a small topic in the wider political landscape, but championed by one of their political allies. When selecting your own frame, be sure to draw on your experience: each of the Republican politicians could be personally united with their angle through either their histories or actions. The masses don't want to see insincere leaders openly pushing what they think will simply get them elected, instead wanting to be fooled into thinking we are sincere. Once the frames were picked, the Republican politicians went into battle with one another, through either direct dialogue or media sparring, to have their frame take precedence in the minds of the voter. The battle was an attempt by each candidate to convince the masses that only they were dealing with the real issue facing society, and that they deserved the public's support at the ballot box.

Once you've selected a frame that successfully unites your person with a predominate issue you need to move to get it legitimised quickly as an important topic worthy of conversation. This is completed by encouraging opposing politicians to discuss your frame, whilst simultaneously avoiding discussion of theirs. To the masses, this will look like you are bringing up important topics worthy of your opponent's attention, while they aren't, as their preferred frame and topics for the election are overtly ignored. The typical rhetoric you should use when another frame is being discussed looks like this.

'Frame B is only a problem because my opponent refuses to deal with Frame A, my frame.'

The defending politician will then have to react to your statement, as, if any part of the masses considers it important, they won't risk alienating themselves from that section of the electorate by ignoring their concerns. The vast majority of the politicians you will be facing believe in the '100%' fallacy, where a politician believes it is possible to attain maximum approval ratings if they get their message right. This is never going to be the case: a left-leaning politician is never going to appeal to the all of the right, nor vice versa, so don't concern yourself with getting involved in other frames that risk exposing a weakness, just focus on the promotion of yours.

Donald Trump was an expert at this, focusing totally on immigration. When other politicians attacked him he shot down those topics and refocused attention on the wall, going to so far as to physically wave away Jeb Bush trying to attack him on 'eminent domain', where he had abused the law to try and poach land from homeowners unwilling to sell.

Any discussion of other people's frames is dangerous. The fate of Hillary Clinton during the presidential election can be attested to the fact that she defended herself from Republican attacks over her private email server when she was accused of using it for confidential communications, presenting a security risk. Instead of pushing the accusations aside, declaring that it was a nonsense her enemies were falsifying, she actively defended herself. By doing this, she accepted the opposition's frame and, as soon as she engaged with it, they closed the gates behind her and started telling everyone she couldn't be trusted with security, whilst they were fighting the 'War on Terror' (something which has seemingly never ended for Republican campaign managers). The same fate befell the United Kingdom's New Labour leader Ed Miliband during the 2015 UK election. His political opponents attempted to cast him as a weak leader, but as opposed to ignore the charge, Miliband made to every attempt to show himself as strong, in one instance getting laughed at by a TV audience when trying to convince a talk show host he was tough. He was also mocked for eating a bacon sandwich, which shows you how hard the masses will go to berate a politician who does not match their frame.

A frame is only important once a conversation starts: by ignoring a damaging frame you simply starve it of oxygen, limiting its appeal. Instead, just focus on the promotion of your own. During the 1984 US election campaign, a 73-year-old Ronald Reagan defended himself from the 'age' question by telling an audience during a debate that he wouldn't make an issue of age during the campaign, regardless of his opponent's youth and inexperience, drawing laughs from everyone present, including the opposing politician, Walter Mondale. This was enough to put the matter to bed and Reagan collected 58.8% of the vote through his other campaign work and went on to become the oldest person to hold the presidential office, the age frame rarely being brought up again. This is by far the most effective tactic, turn an attack into a positive sound bite and move on, if your opponent keeps on attacking it will make them seem petty, repeating their catchphrases whilst the masses watch you discuss more important topics.

It's worth noting here that we see many politicians use an outsider frame, claiming they can bring new ideas to the table, but don't be fooled into thinking this is an effective campaign frame on its own merit. Donald Trump and Bernie Sanders both ran outsider campaigns, but the former was a billionaire businessman trying to get the nomination of a political party that puts a lot of stock in capitalism and the free market, whilst the latter had been part of the country's political establishment since 1979 both as an independent and as part of the Democratic party. Within parliamentary politics, where parties take precedence over individualism, it's rare for such a politician to get much oxygen, normally hidden away on the outer edge of the political spectrum where they can safely yell at clouds, but within the Presidential system, particularly the primaries, we do see outsiders get airtime.

A true outsider has no political experience and builds their frame on this, hoping people vote for blind change as opposed to thoughtful planning. The rhetoric of the outsider politician is always 'I'm not part of the establishment' or 'we need fresh thinking', and that they are the only ones who can provide such a thing. The ideas behind the phrases are good, but a successful politician will always have the qualifications to prove they can deliver. The masses still value effective leadership over promise and charisma – the one small requirement they still maintain is that the politician has the ability to deliver on the promises they make. Carson held significant approval ratings during the early part of his campaign where the masses cast him as the protest vote, polling second behind Trump at some points. However, as time moved on, and his political credentials started to be questioned, there was a significant drop in support as the masses didn't want to risk actually handing him a position where he would have any impact on their lives. The changes in the wider world have not yet got to a point where the masses are willing to support a candidate with no relevant experience, presenting too much of a risk to their futures, so if you do intend to run as a pure outsider, you are best off rethinking your career choice.

Having united the frame with your person, a popular, and easy, way of encouraging the discussion of your frame whilst drawing the focus away from others is to partake in policy extremism. To attract attention, you simply overstate the solution. Recent examples are the building of a wall on the USA/Mexico border, Le Pen's call for an Islamic immigration ban in France, UK Labour Leader Jeremy Corbyn arguing for the nationalisation of certain British Transport divisions and, in Italy, the 5 Star movement running on the promise of cutting parliamentary salaries by 80%. By stating an extreme policy, you encourage your opposition to focus on your solution rather than on the problem itself. Even if 90% of the dialogue between you and the opposition is them disparaging you, it doesn't matter: on voting day your opposing politicians are only worth one vote each, and the time spent attacking you is time not spent shoring up their own support. The masses who are watching the exchange will see a group of politicians arguing over a problem where only one is offering a solution, regardless of how extreme that solution may be.

The UK saw this tactic with the rise of UKIP, an anti-European Union political party, who developed a two pronged attack within their frame of immigration. The basic argument UKIP use to push their frame is that immigrants take up the jobs needed by the country's own nationals, and that this overpopulation of the country not only leads to higher unemployment, but also drains the welfare services and puts a strain on the government to look after its own people in their time of need.

Employment is an important policy area for all political parties and is the first bastion of hope against the government-destroying problem of poverty, yet, for people who have secure employment, or are qualified enough to be able to find work, it's not an urgent problem and therefore won't impact their voting habits. Opposing political parties will also have differing policies to deal with this frame and, effective or not, they can argue the point that immigration is not the problem but other, more solvable, aspects of society are, such as tax breaks for companies or relaxing import/export laws. UKIP, however, follow their unemployment frame by arguing that the lax border controls caused by EU membership also allow criminals into the country unchecked. The frame here then moves from important to urgent. The average member of the masses may have secure employment, but becoming a victim of crime is seen as random chance, with the probability of you being a victim increasing if there are more criminals in the country. The immigration frame is now an urgent problem that needs to be dealt with in a decisive manner. While the other parties may be able to solve the unemployment problem, only UKIP will stop the 'foreign crime wave' with its tough, bordering on extreme, policies. This increased the radicalism of the other parties who, in an attempt to match UKIP's rhetoric to steal their votes, soon started to adopt tougher policies. This is the second advantage of policy extremism: it allows you to set an impossible standard for your opponents to try to match.

You should be marketing your frame as if it is dealing with the most important issue facing society, and by providing an extreme solution to the problem you force opposing politicians into a difficult position. If your opponents do agree your frame is important, they either have to match your solution, officially making you the authority on the subject, or offer another alternative more befitting their station. Doing this is a risk to them, as it will make them look like they are not taking the issue seriously enough for the masses, who would have already decided how urgent the problem is and the solution they prefer, with the lack of time they have in their lives meaning it is generally the first one they hear. The reason for this is that the pure avalanche of information that the masses have to deal with on a day-to-day basis won't allow them enough time to look into each solution offered to a problem; instead, they will use the first solution they hear as a measuring stick, judging any other policy by that standard. This is why it is also important to build a narrative into your frame, explaining to the masses how it fits into their world and why only you hold the answers. The opposing politicians will then have to work that narrative into their response for their response to make sense, legitimising it to the masses and putting you at the head of the conversation. With the changes in how the masses receive their news, it's important as well to ensure the main point of your frame can fit into a headline, on Facebook and Twitter they tend to be effective between 10 and 15 words, if they are marketed urgently enough to catch the reader's eye.

In the unlikely case that a politician tries to outdo you and go more extreme, there is no need to panic: they will look amateurish and unoriginal, simply presenting themselves as a knock-off version of you. Marco Rubio fell victim to this during the 2016 Republican primaries, promising to 'build a wall that works' in order to undercut Trump, a somewhat baffling statement that couldn't be backed up in any real manner. On the other hand, if they argue that your frame is unimportant, and your solution extreme, they risk alienating anyone who is sympathetic to your cause, making them look ignorant on the subject, weakening their support amongst the masses as well as their allies who will worry about their own polling numbers dwindling, due to their backing of a leader seen as weak.

Through the implementation of policy extremism, UKIP, with a focus on immigration and crime being solved with a blanket ban on immigration, saw their vote increase from 4,833 votes in 1997 up to 3,881,129 in 2015. Other parties were seen as either appeasing or ignoring the perceived problems, allowing the party to fulfil its goal of getting the UK to leave Europe through the Brexit referendum of 2016.

All policy areas can be designed in such a manner using policy extremism, so when developing your frame ensure that it has an attached sense of urgency, waking the masses from their slumber to focus on your sales pitch. Environmentalism should be led with catastrophe, not global warming; security should be led with terrorism, not the efficiency of the judiciary system; immigration should be led with crime rather than the job market. An urgent problem will benefit the politician who is willing to solve it, disparaging those with other priorities. The masses no longer have the time, nor interest, to fully research each policy area that will be debated during an election, nor read every newspaper article, so situations will always be as urgent as you say they are. If you are fighting politicians with moderate frames, up the ante of yours to cast them into the shadows.

Promising to ban immigrants, declare a war, cut politicians' salaries by or build a wall are incredibly bold steps to take, and in some cases unworkable, and although you may feel put off by leading with some of these policies – particularly the pay cut – you don't need to be sincere. Post-election there will be plenty of opportunities to cast these policies aside, you will be able to either blame bureaucracy for the inability to carry out a promise, as the masses have always suspected, or have your insider supporters not vote on the matter so it fails to get through either your parliament or congress. The masses that supported you will blame the existing systems of government, freeing you of your obligations, whilst your opposition will be glad to not see it carried out; in both cases you can move on from the promise swiftly, focusing your attention on other more pressing matters. A wall is yet to be built on the United States/Mexican border and it is unlikely to rear its head again until Trump seeks re-election, his supporters blaming Mexico for not paying for it, and the Democrats for everything else.

The reason framing works as an effective political strategy is that the political game is zero-sum. Any vote placed for you cannot be given to another candidate, so any success you have is automatically to the detriment of your opponents. Framing focuses the attention of the masses on a particular subject, lessening the impact felt if you are weaker in other areas. As a working example, in a room of 100 voters, 2 candidates are battling for election and are arguing their policy positions over a wide range of issues. Without a frame, the masses' focus is distributed almost equally across the board: they don't have the time to investigate every topic so will treat them all equally, then side with the politician who wins them over in the most areas. So if one politician is a strong on trade, but weak in other areas, they are almost guaranteed a loss. For example:

	Security	Trade	Immigration	Environment	Total Votes
Politician's votes	0	30	0	0	30
Opponent's votes	30	0	30	10	70
Interest of the masses	30%	30%	30%	10%	100%

However, if the same politician focuses on creating, and getting accepted, a frame on trade, that the country is on the brink of an economic collapse due to poor commercial relations, they can draw interest towards this single topic and coerce the voting patterns:

	Security	Trade	Immigration	Environment	Total votes
Politician's votes	0	75	0	0	75
Opponent's votes	10	0	10	5	25
Interest of the masses	10%	75%	10%	5%	100%

The politician, on a policy by policy basis, is still taking the same number of defeats across the board, but the victory on trade is significant enough that they are irrelevant to the election result. This is why the most effective frames are best based on a policy that is supported by a strong narrative as you can provide a clear solution to the electorate which appeals to their worldview. A frame simplifies the election for the masses, and allows them to focus on a limited number of subjects that will benefit the politician with the strongest frame.

That said, it is possible to create a frame which stretches further than just one individual policy – but do be aware of the pitfalls.

For her run at the 2017 presidency, Hillary Clinton chose not to frame her campaign on any particular issue, but instead on the full continuance of the Obama administration. The sitting president, Barack Obama, was a popular leader and had kick-started big projects, such as the Affordable Care Act ('Obamacare'), which required either completing or defending. Yet instead of picking one of these projects to frame and focus on, she instead framed the election on giving people the choice of voting for the incumbent government for a third term. Her frame gave her no foundation to build a solution to any particular problem, or act as a launch pad for new ideas. Instead what she found was that she would not only have to defend herself from attack, but also the last 8 years of government, regardless of whether she had been instrumental in all its capacities. The opposition party, the Republicans, were therefore able to go on the attack consistently, easily finding distractions or irrelevancies to weaken her moves whenever she looked to build up any momentum. Her opponents, when she did then try to bring up any specific policy area, simply returned focus to her original frame and asked 'Why didn't she fix it over the last few years?' Every policy area she fought for could be combatted with this, leaving the masses open to question both her ability and desire to do the work she promised. This is the same fate that befell John Major in 1997, who asked people to put their faith in the Conservative party as a whole, allowing Labour to pick apart any area they wanted before running off and focusing on something else, their guerrilla politics keeping the conversation moving, limiting the time the Tories had to effectively answer any criticism.

This is not to say it is impossible to create a frame that reaches further than a single policy. Major's opponent, Tony Blair, framed the 1997 UK election on the creation of the modern left, with wide-ranging principles which touched on all aspects of the state. Despite its reach, the message presented by New Labour was still tight – 'New ideas vs bad ideas' – forcing the Conservatives to defend themselves from criticism, but not allowing them to alienate and attack any particular aspect of Labour's manifesto. John Major's confused defence, 'They are copying us, and they are dangerous' led to his defeat;

Hillary Clinton being pulled forced to defend every square meter Obama's 8 year administration led to hers.

The benefit of limited frames is that the politician basing their frame on a situation can offer a solution today. By asking them to back a frame based on a person or a party we are offering the masses the opportunity to put someone in office who can deal with problems that may arise in the future, something they don't put a lot of stock in. They want a quick or limited exchange of goods, wanting to exile us from their political lives as soon as possible, and certainly before we can carry out the presumptive inevitable betrayal they believe is coming.

Due to the change in how the masses deal with the political class's post-Iraq War, frames are most effective when they are aimed at the voter on a rational level. This isn't to say that each policy should be a tax cut, but that the frame should be able to be explained in simple, relatable, terms that can be easily delivered. The voter acts on a cost-benefit analysis, it being easier to draw direct comparisons on that level, so by breaking it down into cash it's easier for the masses to relate to. For example, here are two housing policies to make it easier for people to get on the property ladder

1) Build more houses
2) Drop property taxes for first time buyers

The first policy will lead to the devaluation of the market making it cheaper to buy, but the changes to the prices can't be guaranteed as it depends on how the market reacts. Secondly, the people who own houses are worried about the devaluation of their property, probably their biggest investment, so you risk losing their vote. With the second policy you can attach a firm price: if it's a £1000 saving, you can guarantee that to people, and the masses will take this guaranteed £1000 over a larger, but speculative, figure.

Consider the case for socialized healthcare in the United States. Healthcare is a hot topic, with two separate approaches being heralded by the opposing teams on the left and right of the political spectrum. The argument from the right is to expand the free market in order to increase competition between insurance providers, leading to a drop in the price the individual will spend on coverage. The left, for their part, tend to want a European model where there is a tax increase in order to cover the cost of the healthcare system and the removal of mandatory private insurance. The two models mainly compete over cost, with supporters of privatised medicine arguing that no one should be forced to cover the cost of someone else's healthcare, whilst supporters of social healthcare believe their model will decrease the cost across the board for everyone. Privatised medicine has consistently come out on top in the argument, as they have successfully managed to convince the masses that socialized medicine means tax hikes, regardless of any reduction in insurance premiums.

Democrat Bernie Sanders, who ran against Hillary Clinton during their parties presidential primaries, combatted this by placing a figure on healthcare savings, arguing that socialized healthcare would put $5000 into the pocket of every American, based on the difference between the tax increase and the reduction of insurance premiums. By any standards $5000 a year is a significant saving, around 10% of the average American salary. This meant for the average voter, the sum of money was directly relatable in their minds: low enough that they could mentally spend it, but high enough that it would draw their attention.

The policy also worked by shifting its focus. In the USA, 33 million are without healthcare, about 10.3% of the masses. Previously, socialised medicine focused on this percentage, as they were the ones who would benefit from the increased coverage, essentially asking the rest of the population to make an ethical choice on the subject rather than a rational one. Sanders changed the rhetoric of the argument to focus on the savings that the insured population would be able to make: now 89.7% of the population stood to gain. The shifting of the focus meant that not only did the right wingers now need to increase the coverage of healthcare to match Sander's polices, but also to deliver a $5000 saving to the masses, which would be a very tough task without significant changes to their ideals.

The majority of the policies you may want to enact will focus more toward your inner and social circles, and a shift in target will allow you to achieve your goals. For example, 'trickle-down economics' reduced taxes for the wealthy, whilst being framed that it was actually good for the average citizen: the ultra-rich buying more products from the middle classes with their new disposable income. In fact, the middle classes would be lucky to pick up the oats that fell from the horse's mouth, as the ultra-rich put their new money into portfolios, only increasing their own worth. The reverse of this is why it's best not to back a policy aimed at a minority: the unemployed poor may require welfare, but whilst they represent fewer than 10% of the population they lack the voting power to incentivise us to support them, outside of a rare morality crisis that impacts the middle class, who tend to blame the circumstances of the poor on their life choices as opposed to poor choices in social policy.

The framing of the early campaign is the most important part of the election, as it's the first opportunity you will have to put yourself forward to the masses, who have ignored you for an extended amount time, and start canvassing their vote.

The final four weeks before an election, however, is when your campaign will take on a life of its own. You'll be dragged from town to town, city to city, and region to region to offer those in attendance of your events a rundown of who you are, what you stand for and how effective you will be.

Thus far this self-help guide has ran your through each of these topics in a manner that should allow you to portray yourself in the right light throughout your campaign, however, in the final four weeks, you are much more reliant on the media who will become super interested in the stories they can create about you, rather than the policies you are pushing. This is the time you are most in danger of having your political career destroyed as both media and public scrutiny are at their highest and supporters of your opposition will seek to jump on any opportunity to prove they were right about you all along as they to canvass your potential voters. The time restraints on the 4 weeks before the election also mean that you shouldn't waste time replaying the movie of your political life, instead provide the masses a with a trailer, an all action run through of slogans, photo opportunities, attacks on your opposition and hand shaking, that pumps up the audiences adrenaline and keeps them on the path toward the right choice in the ballot box.

Your strategy should primarily be based on areas you want to swing in your favour, working with the zero sum idea that the votes that come to you can't go to your opposition. Most elections will come down to a small amount of swing states or regions, and managing these along with your resources is the key to victory, so don't worry about sacrificing one area in order to save another, if a small sacrifice in one place, will lead to success in a multitude of others. In the 2016 election Trump pulled out of Virginia, a state that had consistently voted Republican in order to focus on other areas, despite that his opponent had highlighted it as a target state. At the time this seemed like madness, Virginia was for the first time leaning democrat and traditionally this would have made it a battleground state, if only to save face for the Republican nominee who wouldn't want the first one in generations to drop it to the enemy. Instead, Trump removed the resources that would have been spent there and put them into Florida, Pennsylvania and Ohio, allowing him to put more time into those states than he would have been able to otherwise. The Republican strategists knew that Clinton, regardless of Trumps appearances in the state, would have to put a concerted amount of effort into the state to turn it, so as opposed to fight her, they allowed her to waste her resources. Clinton kept putting the work into the state, hoping to so comprehensively defeat Trump across the board that the Virginian victory would simply be a victory lap to cap off her monumental rise to power. Instead, the 8 days she spent winning the state, was 8 days she wasn't shoring up support in the areas that Trump moved his focus to, and won.

There are three keys to a good frame: urgency, solution, and relatable narrative. A frame without urgency is unimportant, a frame that is unrelatable is unrequired, and a frame without a solution is ineffective. Trump, New Labour and UKIP compete across the political spectrum but through applying effective frames, they were able to control the conversation and make promises to the masses that the opposition were either unwilling or unable to match. They maintained control of the conversation, targeted a particular policy area and kept their message tight, running a campaign of offence that forced their opposition to legitimise the conversation. When attacked, they shifted the focus back onto their own frame, not allowing any damaging information to spend too long in daylight, casting any advantage an opponent had as a distraction from the real problem. Despite glaring weaknesses, Trump, Labour and UKIP all saw electoral success, whilst Clinton, Major and Carson are now footnotes in wider political stories.

Frame your campaign, and reap the rewards.

Building the Brand

The biggest challenge to the up-and-coming politician is that recent social trends have left us disliked by the masses who now see us as empty suited shills for corporate interests or whiney sycophants begging for votes. If you fall into this trap, the masses may reject you and your frame before you get a chance to properly engage with them. Menzies Campbell, Michael Howard and Ed Milliband all fell at the first hurdle, not fitting the masses' ideal of what a politician should look like, whilst Chris Christie, Paul Nuttall and Ben Carson had their careers ended as they didn't suit the voter's idea of how they should behave. It therefore becomes important for you to build an aura around yourself that lets the masses know that they are going to want to listen to whatever it is you say, prior to you actually having to say it.

In times past, politicians would attempt to achieve this by uniting themselves with an ideology, an all-encompassing political philosophy that presented a collection of shared beliefs which sought to coherently explain the world in which we live, why problems exist and what solutions we can apply to fix them. The two main ideologies of the 20th century, socialism and liberalism, had generous support from the masses across the Western world who saw them as adequate explanations for their lot in life. As a result these ideologies became important to politicians seeking to signpost to the voting population which side of the philosophic coin they were on, and what could be expected of them once in power.

The goal of throwing their support behind an ideology was so that the politician would convince the masses that they were allies, and that success for them would equate to a shared reward. Ideologies for their part appealed to the masses by working top down, applying a value to each member of society in order to distinguish their usefulness in the achievement of its goals. For example, an ideology that strives to increase industrial output will place more value on hard workers than lazy ones; a racial ideology in contrast still places value on lazy workers if they have the right skin colour, devaluing those of a different genetic background instead. This valuation, if high enough, is an invitation to the party and a share in any rewards that are reaped: if a communist utopia is realised, all the workers are rewarded with power and riches; if the racists win their supporters no longer have to live with the supposedly 'inferior' races. Because of this, people would only subscribe to an ideology if they felt valued and are therefore able to benefit from its success, the rich were unlikely to vote for socialist politicians at the risk of losing their capital, whilst entrepreneurs would throw their support behind the liberal cause, hoping for more freedoms in the quest for more profit. By putting themselves near the top of the ideological tower, politicians could easily attain the masses' investment for their own political gain acting as the harbinger for their eventual reward.

The help ideologies gave the politician was not, however, without cost. From a practical stand point, the difficulty in ideologies is that they can be seen as both dictatorial and elitist. The roadmap leading to utopia isn't so much a hand guide as it is a set of instructions passed down from on high – there is a right way to behave, and a right way to think. Ideologies kept a tight control on the political message, limiting the amount a politician could stray from the path, regardless of how well they were polling. The competition from other ideologies, in a zero-sum system where there were a limited number of votes to be shared, put politicians in the difficult position of choosing between sticking on message, or adapting it in order to find more success, but then running the risk of being cast out by their allies and heralded a traitor to the cause. This meant that a lot of politicians became tied to ideologies that were detrimental to their chances of success, sacrificing their long term flexibility in order to earn a starting place in the political game.

This ideological programming, enforced upon those choosing to play the game, acted as a management tool for the political parties who sought to further control us, constricting the individual's actions through direct orders relating to our behaviours. By signing up to an ideology, we politicians were signalling to the rest of our potential allies that we were willing to play ball, pushing the party's message over one of our own, allowing the upper echelon of the party to encircle and cast out those of us simply chasing our own ends. During his early career, Tony Blair's renown as a member of the soft left made it hard for him to find a local party in the hard left North of the United Kingdom that would nominate him for a seat in which to stand for election, as the hardliners rallied round their own, unsure of where his allegiances truly lay. Upon his rise to Labour leadership, Blair's centrist 'Third Way' ideology, understanding that turn around was fair play, committed to the same course of action, alienating those who held in high regard the old ideologies, offering only the strongest adherents token positions in the new order, whilst alienating the rest to the backbench.

Due to its monopoly it held on the access to the political game, ideology remained an incredibly strong facet of the politician's life. Not only this, but the duopoly of socialism and liberalism allowed the masses to split the world simply into two opposing teams, the Left and the Right, matching the rhetoric of the on-going Cold War. For the political classes, this left few options on where to place our loyalty and we would end up constricted in our behaviours and actions, essentially making us the local spokesperson for other people's ideas. But that was the price of admission to the great game.

In the modern world, however, the information age and the rise of the internet have changed the way the masses interact with their world. The grip ideology had on politicians, and therefore the political system, was seemingly indestructible, yet the outbreak of the Iraq War and the collapse of the old political/media alliances soon broke it away from the everyday lives of the masses. The NSMs saw ideology as one of the hallmarks of the old political system and their supporters, no longer trusting in one world view to answer every question, could use the accessibility of the internet to engage with hundreds of different ideologies, with each referring to only one aspect of society, without considering themselves hypocritical. Thanks to the internet, each motivated member of the public now has the ability to do their own research, find holes in any ideological roadmap that a politician might lay out, then through the expansion of social media, broadcast it to the masses in an attempt to disrupt any support they have. The era of one size fits all model of political thought has come to an end.

With this change, most modern politicians quickly distanced themselves from the traditional ideologies, knowing that it would be them who bore the brunt of the masses' fickle anger against the faceless philosophies which had been selling them lies in exchange for a duopoly of power. The politicians who remained loyal to the old system were ousted as shills, ideology becoming a by-word for lazy in the political world, used to disparage those who hadn't properly thought through their plans and were just running through the motions of a belief system they held no real connection too. Both sides of the political spectrum started decrying their opponent's plans as 'ideologically driven', now utilising the selective membership of philosophies to push onto the masses that it would be their friends that got rewarded, not the commoner.

With the masses no longer considering themselves as part of an ideological belief system, politicians became free to abandon its shackles and chase their own ends, useful in an era where flexibility on morality and policy is important in maintaining our position and the attention of the masses. In this world, where the voter can be just as informed on all key policies as a governmental minister, it's important to move past ideology and into the world of political branding. Time can be spent battling for an ideology and explaining to the masses why a certain set of ethical, progressive or economic steps must be taken to ensure the greatest outcome, but the time spent doing this is time lost in the fight to win an election when facing politicians who are more than happy to pander to the masses to garner their support. Instead, we must focus on the creation of brands which tend to be much more time-effective, as you can avoid presenting actual ideas and instead focus on wide-eyed ideals that appeal to everybody.

Pre-Tony Blair, the United Kingdom's Labour party was part of what is now considered the socialist 'Old Left', with the cornerstone of their five-yearly manifestos being workers' rights, set out in 'Clause IV' of the party's constitution. Old Labour's political ideology could essentially be broken down into the following statement:

'Worker's rights are protected through the engagement between the Trade Unions and the Bosses. Group bargaining protects the Worker from abuses'

From this we can see part of the socialist ideological roadmap: unionise the workers and allow them leverage in the workplace so they can protect themselves from greedy bosses.

The socialist ideology therefore put value on trade unionists and their supporters, who would reap the reward of a better bargaining position, and therefore better wages. During the 1970s, trade union membership in the UK peaked at 12 million, and the four elections held during this time saw the Labour party return 12.2 million votes in 1970, 11.6 million in February 1974, 11.4 million in October 1974 – all under Wilson – before falling out of power in 1979, returning 11.5 million under James Callaghan and losing out to Thatcher's 13.5 million.

The defeat to Thatcher, and the following decade of weakening trade union support following their disruptive behaviours, saw many members of the Labour party devaluing the stock of the old left's ideology. By the time Tony Blair took over the leadership of the party, there were just over 6 million trade union members and the previous leadership had alienating the wider voting population by seeking out special treatment for their valued members through successive strikes and industrial action. This made Old Labour's ideology dangerous for those politicians seeking to remain employed. The 'valued' members of society would deliver, as they had in the past, but their weight in support was now only 6 million, much lower than it had been previously and significantly less than what was needed. Had Old Labour run in the election of

1997 they would have needed to find another 3 million votes outside of the unions to beat the Conservatives, a feat that the old left had never achieved. With this in mind, Tony Blair's New Labour updated Article 5 and distanced themselves from the trade unions. Now separated in rhetoric from the trade unions, New Labour's ideology could be broken down into a simple statement

'Workers' rights are important'

No roadmap, no plan, but also no questions. Workers' rights here could literally mean anything: more pay, more job security, or not getting beaten with chains, so there's nothing for the voter to disagree with. It's a safe assumption that almost the entire working population will want some essence of 'workers rights', allowing New Labour to apply value to the entirety of society, without giving up their 'ideology'.

The working population in the UK in 2018 sits at 26 million, and every single one of them can now buy into, or at least relate to, Labour's new 'vision'. This is part of the reason why internal divisions have appeared within Labour since the election of new leader Jeremy Corbyn, a member of the hard left and supporter of the unions. His move back to placing preferential value on traditional trade union support threatened to alienate the non-unionised working force, reducing support back to just the guaranteed 6 million, and entering a battle with the Conservative party for the rest. Corbyn, to protect his own position, built on the Trade Union foundation, which he could guarantee would turn out to vote for him, and aimed the majority of his campaign at the youth, knowing the traditional young Liberal vote had abandoned their party after the 2010 coalition government where they were linked to the Conservative's austerity programs. Corbyn offered the young and the alienated a political home, where he could build on the guaranteed 6 million trade union votes with wider promises made of a better future for the youth, regardless of whether they agreed with all of his stances, particularly on Brexit. Here we saw the impact of NSMs in motion: Corbyn's campaign team did away with the promotion of policy, where he risked losing support, and instead focused on the personality cult surrounding him. Like Tony Blair before him, Corbyn built the 'Young People are our Future' party, placing value on the 23.7 million people aged between 18 and 29, who were unlikely to be Trade Union Members, despite falling on the opposite ideological front to the youth when it came to Europe and Brexit.

Whilst their various supporters will cast the other as the epitome of evil, both Tony Blair and Jeremy Corbyn knew that the brand you build must still define the product you are trying to sell. New Labour, when building their brand, didn't throw out the baby with the bath water by getting rid of the workers along with the trade unions, instead they created the 'Workers' Rights are Still Important' party, though Corbyn for his part still promoted the unions whilst creating the 'Young People are our Future' party. The brands they created to replace the ideologies that threatened to cost them dearly, were still based on the principles of the political supporters they already had, who would overlook major changes to the message in order to maintain the emotional and political investment they have in the party. The masses are unlikely to cut and run from an emotional investment in a politician, as by joining a new political party they have to start at the bottom, making them last in line to collect on any potential reward. They will still feel that the party relates to them, willing turning a blind eye to evidence that suggests otherwise, whilst you expand your message to include other potential voters. Had Labour completely abandoned the workers to become a libertarian party, other parties on the hard left may well have seen their membership surge as the loyalists moved to pastures new.

The centrepiece of designing a brand – particularly for a political party – is personification, and within a capitalist model it makes sense to follow in the footsteps of big business. When asked to describe Nike as a person, people saw them as an athlete with a positive, 'can do' attitude. Their rival Tapout on the other hand was seen as a tough guy. Despite competing in the same field the two rival companies maintain different brands and attract different buyers, and this resonates within the political sphere. In the UK, the Conservative party can be personified as a member of the upper middle class with a good job where money isn't an issue, similar to the Republican Party in the United States. Before the Blair/Brown Revolution, the Labour party was seen as a blue collar, flat cap worker; the development into New Labour was to see them becoming the new middle classes, young and technologically savvy, created by Thatcher's governments. The brands aren't static, a change made by the Conservatives saw them drop their traditional torch from the crest for a cartoon tree to elect a more responsible and environmental tone to their brand. The symbolism of the flat cap worker, for its part no longer needed by New Labour, was picked up by the hard-left parties who wished to resurrect the brand for their own use, hoping to attract more of the disenfranchised to their cause by presenting themselves in the light of the traditional working class.

The flat cap, however, soon found itself co-opted by the British right as a symbol for the traditional shopkeeper and salt of the earth worker, with the lazier politicians of the anti-EU lobby utilising it to link themselves to the mythical era when the UK operated separate from the rest of the world. By wearing it they are signalling to the watching masses of not only their political stance, but the narrative they are peddling. The majority of these politicians came from non-traditional backgrounds so the cap not only gives them an entry point into the minds of the masses prior to verbally engaging with them, but it also allows them leeway in their style. These politicians could make mistakes, or express outlandish beliefs, but as opposed to be a mark against their amateurism, it instead became an enduring part of their honesty, something the masses thrived for following their collapse in trust with the traditional political classes. It's the same reason politicians choose wear their party colours: it allows them an all-access pass to the viewer and exceptions for any mistakes they may make from their supporters. The strength of the symbolism behind the flat cap is not only relatable to the 'working class' politician, but it can be used successful to unite any voting base if plied correctly. Donald Trump's "Make America Great Again" hats represents a fantastic understanding of how important imagined communities are to the voter.

The hat, normally bright red, when worn in public acts as an overt sign to which way the wearer intends to vote. When other supporters of Trump see it signals to them that the wearer will defend their beliefs in the ballot box, and is therefore an ally. In their day to day lives, each Red Hat they spot on the street lends further credence to the voter that they are a part of a community much bigger than themselves and, as in all community settings, they will soon start to build relationships with other adherents, creating support networks and activist groups all focused on the promotion and protection of their group. The creation of a community in this manner not only shores up your own support by creating a welcoming home for new adherents, it also makes it much harder for them to leave, as they would now not only be turning away from you, but every community relationship they have cultivated. The Red Hats soon became one of Trumps strongest marketing tools, not only did they create a community of voters he could rely on to vote for him, but the abuse handed down by the oppositions supporters upon seeing the hat, mixed with the publicity that could be made of such incidents over social media, only further convinced his supporters they had nowhere else to turn as no other social group wanted them, once in the Trump gang, you were in for life.

Rally's also operate in this manner, and are a fantastic tool if you can use them correctly, the correct manner being a pure advertisement of numbers. The idea of a mass gathering of supporters is to not only advertise the popularity of the politician, but to remind the masses sitting at home of their obligations towards their community as they see all people like them giving out so much energy in the support of their hero. This further reminds them that the politician they have chosen to support has a large following, legitimising their faith in them, as well as, advertising to those at home the preferred behaviours of the politician's supporters, be loud, be proud, and be there. Plenty of politicians mix up rally's for photoshoots and try to combine the two with backdrops of the topic they are discussing, whether it's having workers in high visibility jackets or nurses as they explain their policy positions toward a line of cameras. All this does is provide an artificial backdrop, devoid of any relatable reality where a politician is lecturing cameras about a subject that is behind them. It does little to promote the politician as a leader, and a lot to promote them as distant from the real problems and the people experiencing them.

The creation and marketing of these brands mean that it is easier for people to make assumptions on the party's policies, as if they can directly them to the brand, they will assume its relatable to themselves. It's therefore changed how people choose their political parties.

Under the system of ideology, parties would stress the roadmap, and then it would be up to voters to decide if it seemed like a good plan before they threw their support behind the party that embodied it. We want to escape this, as in the modern world the voter may well find flaws in any plan you put forward, so instead we want to create an empathetic brand that's easier to relate too. Once we have an empathic relationship with the masses we can evolve it into an 'us v them' mentality, where they will dismiss arguments coming from other sides as a direct attack on what they believe, invoking a passionate reaction they will take to the streets. The difference on how voters interpret political ideologies and brands can be seen below

Ideology	Brand
Voter aware of the party	Voter aware of the party
Party puts forward its ideological roadmap	Party puts forward its brand
Voter decides if they believe in the ideology	Voter decides if the brand is relatable to them
Party announces its policies	Party announces its policies
Voter decides if they think the policies match their interpretation of the ideological roadmap	Voter reinterprets the brand to match the policies
Voter interprets policy on what they know of the party	**VOTES**
VOTES	

A brand, if enacted correctly, has a much smaller failure rate than an ideology as its flexibility will allow people with widely different interpretations of policy convince themselves it fits in with the brand they identify with. Ideology relies on the masses' trust of the politician to enact policy; a brand only asks that the voter trust in the kind of people they keep company with. It's no longer up to the party to convince the voter to support them, it's for the voter to continually convince themselves.

A brand works to illicit a different response from the voter than an ideology or a political platform. The latter asks the voter to actively engage with a part of society that they may be unfamiliar with, and this means they have to put their trust in the politician as a guide. Presenting a problem or policy first means the politician will always be judged by the standard set by the situation and their ability to work within those confines. With the collapse in trust post-Iraq War, this is unlikely to work out favourably for them. Instead, a brand introduces the masses to the politician first and aims to make them relatable, which means when a situation arises or the politician wants to push a policy, the masses will instead ask themselves if the imaginary vision they have of the politician has the ability to succeed. A good brand will make sure the response is always positive.

As an individual politician, it's also important that you also maintain a brand separate from the party, so people know what to expect from you outside of the collective message. Your brand should be in keeping with the message the party is pushing – there aren't many Marxists leading conservative parties – but your personal brand should be based on your own experiences and the properties that are naturally attached to your past. If you are a former military leader, present yourself as such. The brand is how we are going to start to build the illusion of trust with the masses, so their first impression of you shouldn't be of someone who has abandoned their foundations to create something different as they will see this as a risk. Where you have come from should be integral to your brand as a politician.

It's also important to only act within the confides of the brand: a military leader who all of a sudden starts posing with puppies or kissing babies will lose votes, as the brand is compromised and people will be confused about the message, eroding trust. The 2016 US election saw Donald Trump take on Hillary Clinton. Trump, throughout the election, presented himself as a passionate, honest, 'outsider' politician with business credentials. All his actions were tied to this brand, from his outspokenness to his conservative values. Hillary, on the other hand, moved from career politician, to 'Grandma knows best', to strong leader, to the true successor of Barack Obama and so forth. The constant movement of her brand meant that people weren't sure what stance she was taking on any particular topic, leading to people distrusting her as they were unable to relate any part of her policies to a stable brand that they felt truly represented her. If Google started openly designing nuclear missile software in the face of its company mission statement 'Don't be evil', the goodwill it built with its brand would take a big hit as people began to question the companies true motives, simply judging them by the rules they had set themselves. Sticking to the brand allows us to avoid this issue as people will simply judge us by what they expect of the brand and a good marketer will be able to protect themselves from any blowback they may get from a bad policy.

An effective brand will therefore cover the gap between who you are and what you are selling. It will demonstrate the values you hold and how they impact the decisions you make, allowing you to push all manner of policies, regardless of whether they contradict one another. A strong brand will allow a politician on the right of the spectrum to push leftist policies and vice versa, as their supporters will convince themselves that it fits in with the brand they support. A politician with an army background cutting the military spending can be acceptable, if their brand is about efficiency and cutting waste. Another benefit is that people, if they are unfamiliar with a policy area, will support any movement a politician makes if they believe in strongly enough in their brand, the model of trust covering the gap in knowledge the individual may have.

Upon attaining power you must be aware, however, that the brand you cultivate will always expand beyond your control, with supporters developing certain expectations of you if you don't keep a tight grip on its development. During the UK's European Referendum vote, a significant percentage of the 'out' vote expected that if they won, all immigrants would be thrown out of the country, something bureaucratically and politically impossible, as well as economically suicidal. As no 'out' politician explained that wouldn't be the case for fear of alienating their support, each voter made up their own mind about what 'out' would actually mean, and now hold these politicians accountable to the standards they set themselves. Thus the 'out' vote was soon tied to the brand of anti-immigration and anti-foreign and in order to maintain support, the politicians decided to play ball never expecting to truly win the referendum, but able to use the opportunity to build support for any future attempts at political leadership, note Boris Johnson. When the results came in, they instead found they were now tied to a damaging brand and each of the Brexit leaders ejected themselves from the political process as soon as time would allow, not wanting to be tied to the campaign once it failed to deliver on its promises in the manner the public expected.

To avoid this, although a good brand will sell you to the masses making the rise to power a whole lot easier, you will need to ensure that it is constantly managed and that every message delivered is the correct one.

The changes in the wider world have not disturbed what the masses want from their political leaders, and they will actively seek out the benefits each one offers. It's important, therefore, to ensure from day one you highlight the rewards the voter will receive for supporting you. A straight talker will give them honesty, a bureaucrat will give them organisation, and a business person will control the economy. These benefits are essentially your marketing campaign as you put forward the concepts that will make you a successful politician and the right person to lead the country. George W Bush spoke about his time working with both the Democrats and Republicans, casting him as the peacemaker in a polarized political system, Tony Blair put himself at the centre of the reinvention of the Labour party, and Donald Trump used his experience in making deals to convince the population that he was the right person to broker for the country's future. Each had a clear promise on what they intended to deliver, and have been held to those standards, the failing of the 'Out' Campaign was not to manage these expectations, and allow a dumpster fire of half-baked promises and sly nods to decide what was what, lessening their control over any promised outcomes.

It's important to note, that you certainly shouldn't promise any reward that the masses can't relate to your attributes or relies on support that is outside of your control, as this will shorten your stay in the political game, as you will be seen to be essentially making empty promises. During the Republican primaries for the 2016 election, Mr Carson argued the reward in voting for him was that you'd get a 'political outsider' who would shake up the political world. However, this reward was derived from the fact that he was a former brain surgeon, meaning there was no guarantee he could deliver on the promise as he offered no qualifications as to his ability in the political realm. His medical background could have be utilised successfully if he wished to instil humanity into his campaign, but there are very few 'outsiders' in medicine, and those who are, generally are considered 'quacks'. By asking the masses to consider him an 'outsider', he instead invited them to consider him as a quack. His final primary results in New Hampshire put him at 2.3% of the vote having fallen from 2nd favourite in the early stages.

Regardless of the benefits you bring to the table, it is of the utmost importance you have a personality.

The personality of your brand holds much more importance than the other aspects, as the masses are more forgiving to politicians they would happily share a drink with.

Bill Clinton's saxaphone won him the election, Blair's punk band made him relatable, Bush was the cowboy, whilst Obama actively promoted a personal brand that extended beyond his own person. Much like Tony Blair adapted to the change in the way the media handled new reporting, US President Barack Obama did the same with the rise of the internet. The 'bro-romance' between himself and vice-president Joe Biden cast him as relatable to the masses who could see him act not just as a president, but in a more relaxed setting as a down to earth character, and he was quick to take advantage of that. By bringing his wife, Michelle, into the frame he was also able to appeal to the rising NSMs who were looking for relatable people they could hold up as people to emulate, who fell outside of the traditional political realm. Everywhere the Obama's went together, they were inseparable and therefore seen as part of the same operation, but untied to the presidency Michelle Obama was able to link herself to countless charities and groups, acts impossible for Barack himself due to the limitations of the presidential office. Judged as a group the Obama brand grew so strong that, upon the end of the eight-year term, calls went up around the country for Michelle to stand for office in the future, despite holding no political credentials of her own.

The failures of failing to correctly apply personality to the brand ia abundant: Hillary Clinton changed so often she was seen as fickle, Al Gore was boring, and Ed Miliband was socially awkward. The trick with showing personality is not to seem God- esque – nobody wants perfect friends – but to show controllable faults. It's no coincidence that Tony Blair was discovered to be in a bit of a nerdy band; rather it was a carefully managed publicity stunt. People don't want to think that their leaders are better than them.

Being the Best You

Despite being considered one of the defining features of Western civilisation, the concept that democracy is system open to all is a fallacy promoted by those already at the top of the political pyramid in order to add legitimacy to their own position as the 'true representatives' of the masses.

Every other tried and tested political system has seen its leaders live lifestyles far devolved from the lives of their subjects, the Divine Right of Kings never meant they had to work in the fields with the serfs, the various communist experiments lifted formerly working class leaders, such as Mao and Stalin out of poverty and into palaces, and even Latin American Populist movements have tended to err on the side of dictatorship, making the corruption of position seen to be a very human attitude to power. Democracy attempted to fight these accusations off, the representatives are rotated on a regular basis, elections are common fold and most leaders stories start them holding local office before climbing up the party ranks and on to bigger and better things. Still, working class people are incredibly unlikely to hold the highest political offices, in the United States, President Truman (1945-53) was the last not to hold a College degree whereas in the UK John Major (1993-97) and James Callaghan (1976-79) are the only modern UK leaders to achieve the same feat, with only 9 Prime Ministers, total, not coming from fee-paying schools as long as the role has existed. The USA has only seen one President from a minority background, and no women, whilst the UK has had two female leaders, despite the gender represented by 23% of the US Senate, 19.3% of the House of Representatives, and 32% of the United Kingdom's Parliament.

For the common member of the masses then, it seems like an upward battle with none of us being able to control the circumstances of our birth, which is tied so closely to our social class, economic prosperity and even how much support we get during our academic studies from both our teachers and our family. However, it's important to remember that Obama didn't win the presidency because he was black, and Thatcher didn't become Prime Minister because she stood as woman, they won because they knew how to play the political game. Gender, education and ethnicity aren't exclusionary traits, and neither the masses nor your political colleagues are looking to deny you position due to this criteria, instead they are looking for the inclusionary criteria that sets the successful politician aside from the multitude of failures; Networks.

The Labour party has traditionally been seen as the party of the United Kingdom's working classes, but whereas this may be where they garner their support from, it's certainly not from where they chose their leaders nor their representatives. The Labour Party puts a lot of stock in the Trade Unions, with only 3 of their former Prime Ministers not being members of one, however, outside of the party, the Unions are low on political power, representing 6 million people, but only 18% of the countries workforce. In prior eras, when Union membership was higher, the Labour vote could be tracked alongside it, with the vast majority of the Working Class seeking the protection of collective bargaining during the ideological battles of the 1960's, 1970's and 1980's where their rights were on the line. The defeat of the Unions and the stripping of their power has led to the shredding of their membership, even though more and more of the British population consider themselves to be working class, surveyed at 60% in 2016. These changes mean that with Labour returning 12.8 million votes in 2017, the Trade Unions at most were worth only 48.3% of the party's support, despite the fact that 97.4% of the parties MPs needing to seek out explicit Union support to push through their campaigns and selection.

The response of the left is typically that the Trade Unions represent the desires of the working class, regardless of whether they actively support them or not, so although the influence they hold over the party is disproportionate to what they deliver, it's not undue. What it certainly means though, for the pragmatic politician, that as an influencer on position and policy, the Trade Unions are a network that you going to want to utilise to climb the Labour ladder of power, and whilst membership is an average of £20 a month, it's a very small price to pay to shore up their investment in you.

Networking for political power, however, is not the monopoly of the United Kingdom's Labour party, all political parties would much rather pick their leaders from sources they trust. The 6 Prime Ministers the Conservative party has given the United Kingdom since the Second World War have came with an Oxford education, with the only exception, John Major being groomed from the age of 21 by members of the party who saw his potential, but wanted to ensure he fitted the mould they had for their Members of Parliament. You should remain open to these opportunities, you need to promote yourself as a person willing to tow the party line, and that does include walking through doors that have been held open for you. In return, down the line the network, and the people within who supported you will, expect returns though either policy coercion, or career favouritism, but once in control, feel free to ignore these charges as many have in the past. The political players who tend to push others to the front are either are low on their own political power or fear taking on a big position themselves. Because of this, casting them out will have little repercussions for your career, they may well grumble, but they are unlikely to find support in the people they refused to help while pushing you forward, and will generally fade into becoming a historical footnote.

Good networking will also enable you to meet party donors, who are willing to fund your political campaigns, buy you ad space and pay off those looking to disparage you for a quick pay day, in return for influence. However, it important to realise that fundraising is not the driver of success, and plenty of politicians have gone into campaigns with vast amounts of money only to be beaten in the electoral race by their less wealthy opponents. Studies have shown that during repeated contests between the same candidates, the money spent during an election had little, if any, impact on the results. The confusion happens when looking at politics on a grand scale, every winner of a US presidential election since 1968 has spent more than their rival, leading many politicians to see causation where there is only correlation, and this belief can we bend toward our advantage.

Big money donors treat monetary donations as a gamble, and therefore it's prudent of them not to support the politician they think is more likely to support their agenda, but the politicians they think will win the election putting them in a position to return their investment through friendlier policies, whether it be tax breaks for their super wealthy owners, or the promotion of environmental pet projects. The belief that cash brings votes means that many politicians are willing to fall for this ploy, knowing the life cycle of a failed politician is incredibly short, they will gladly pay back double on any favours they receive that they believe put them in office, but it's important to free yourself from this illusion.

Attracting huge sums of money has little to do with your gullibility or how flexible your manifesto may be, but in your ability to attract voters. Like the masses, donors are looking for charisma, reliability, and timing, as these are the things that win elections. Obama attracted huge sums of money, the most of any presidential candidate, not because of the donor's belief that they could corrupt him, but they knew he would win and wanted to be in his good books when it came time design future policy positions. On the other side of the equation, donors made the same mistake as the pollsters when they bet against Trump, whose campaign brought in less money than Romney and George W Bush, with only his Super-

PAC putting him ahead of John McCain's failed presidential bid. Those who did back Trump soon had their faith repaid as he quickly settled his debt, Sheldon Adelson put pressure on the President to move the US Embassy in Israel to Jerusalem, along with the Home Depot CEO who founded the Israel Democracy Institute. Coal Baron Robert Murray saw his loyalty repaid with the presidency rolling back the environmental protections that hamstringed his industry, Robert Wood Johnson, owner of the New York Jets donated $1 million and is now the U.S ambassador to the United Kingdom, whereas Linda McMahon, co-founder of World Wrestling Entertainment, donated $6 million and became the administrator of the U.S Small Business Administration. The truth is, Trump had no need to do this, his lack of funding shows that the money he did receive had little to no impact on the election result, so he could still have chased his own ends, with small concessions as 'thank you notes' rather than large scale policy changes in return for their support.

The power that comes from fund raising and networking can seriously improve your chances in alternative ways, with a large war chest scaring off your poorer competition and the networking depleting the possible support of candidates willing to stand against you, who will not want to risk what could be their only shot at leadership on trying to beat insurmountable odds. Hilary Clinton, not only had a giant war chest but thanks to her bailing out the Democratic National Committee, the governing body of the Democrat party, she shored up her own support network to the point that when she stood for nomination, only 2 others felt it worth standing against her during the primaries, Martin O'Malley, who returned 0.6% of the Iowa state delegates before pulling out, and Bernie Saunders, who appealed to the hard-left of the party and were put off by Hilary Clinton. The Republicans, with no clear favourite, saw a host of politicians willing to gamble their chances, with 17 candidates standing for nomination, offering a much more open field than their competitors.

With both the donors and masses both looking for the 'right' candidate, it's important to get your personal life in line. The vast majority of successful politicians are married, with the recent developments in the tabloid media meaning that every aspect of a politician's life is up for grabs if it can shift enough units. As a potential goldmine in terms of sensationalist headlines, single politicians act as mating call for the media to start digging around in their personal lives looking for dirt. French President Francois Hollande found his personal affairs published on a French website forcing his partner to give up some of her duties as a journalist for *Paris Match,* and it would be another newspaper that would eventually bring this relationship to an end by reporting on his later affair.

Religion is also plays a huge part in the life of the successful politician, but it isn't simply a case of claiming a religious allegiance and waiting for them to carry you to electoral success, more Catholics voted for the Episcopalian George W Bush, then their own John Kerry, and religion has never proven to be a good indicator on which way a person will vote. Even the infamous 'Religious Right', and its perceived importance on the American political system, is not simply a group of Protestant Fundamentalist block voters who vote for whoever yells about God the loudest the most often. Like money, electoral results push tend to influence views one way; only one President has come from a non-protestant background, the Catholic John F Kennedy, and only one Vice-President, Joe Biden. The classic thought is that religious outsiders have struggled to get on board with the religious right in the country and the outliers, JFK and Biden, worked around this. JFK framed his religion as a result of his Irish-Catholic heritage, whereas the rise of Joe Biden came at time when American fears of the Popes involvement in American affairs had been displaced by fears of an Islamic one.

The thought continues that with 71% of Americans identifying themselves as Christian, and 53% saying they would refuse to vote for an Atheist (a number that has only grown over recent years), being a religious preacher in the United States is as much a platform for a president as being a senator. However, as each election rolls around and each presidential candidate stumbles through questions about their own faith, with both Trump and Clinton getting facts about their own religion wrong in the most recent election, it becomes clearer that the masses aren't interested in a candidates own personal relationship with God, but the special relationship between God and their country, and this is the one you need to appeal too in the US political system.

This is the American Civil Religion, and like most religions it has a set of sacred symbols, such as the flag, forefathers in the founding fathers, and even martyrs such as Abraham Lincoln and the Soldiers who died whilst fighting for the American ideals. Whereas your personal religion may not play a big part in getting you elected, your willingness to participate in the civil religion will, so adding terms such as 'fighting for the flag' and 'God Bless America' to your repertoire will certainly aid your career. Bill Clinton acted as a pastor for God at every given moment, and Obama, following his Democrat Predecessors, consistently invoked the relationship between God and country, the Republican side of the political spectrum has also hammered home the special place the US has in Gods heart, with George W Bush telling Palestinian leaders that God sent him to end the tyranny in Iraq.

The role of the President is essential to this civil religion, so as you start out your political career you are going to want to signal to the masses you are willing to fulfil the role. Politicians act as the master of ceremonies, in place of an actual religious leader, and are expected by the masses to embody the relationship through both their speeches and actions, such as leading the pledge of allegiance, which was a cause of worry for many when it was suggested Obama didn't, and being at the forefront of any military parade, which became the focus of Trump's early presidential career. You don't need to be versed in your own religion to carry out the role, just happy to carry out your symbolic duties, and it's telling that religions that have rejected the civil religion are sparsely represented at the top of the political pyramid. The Jewish faith, which considers itself to have its own a special relationship with God, has seen one of its members, Joe Lieberman, run for vice-president with Al Gore, but he so far remains the only one to run for one of the highest offices, despite how strong the Israeli lobby is in American politics. The Unitarians, who reject the idea that religious truth can be laid down by either a holy person or an institution, have also shied away from offering a country any sort of special significance and last had a president, William Howard Taft, in 1913. Even the rejection of Catholics from political system can be tied to the allegiance laid at the feet of the Pope who heads up the religion, a role circled by the American masses for the President.

The 53% of the religious population that would refuse to vote for an Atheist, are not holding out for a politician that matches their belief system, or even has a good knowledge of it. Much like the Catholics would refuse to elect an Atheist as Pope, the religious right simply wants a president that will fulfil the symbolic functions of the countries quasi-religion. This makes it incredibly important to signal to the masses at the first available instance that you are willing to play the role and promote the special American relationship about God.

The American experience with religion and politics, however, is not one you can repeat around the world and expect to be successful. In the UK, religious politicians are viewed with a certain amount of distrust, with the two explicitly religious political parties, the Christian Party and the Christian Peoples Party returning 7589 votes in the last general election, split between their 33 candidates, polling behind the Yorkshire Parties 21 candidates who received a total of 20958 votes despite running in only one region. Even the Church of England, the state religion, has seen itself grow distant from its previous political allies in the conservative party, the religion moving to the political left on social issues, whilst the party maintained its position by on the right. The problems that arise with being an openly religious political party leader can be found in the misadventures of the former leader of the Liberal Democrats, Tim Farron.

Prior to him taking over the reins of the party, the Liberal Democrats had entered a significant down period, coming off the back of a coalition government where they had been forced to give up the promises they had made, including ones to their strong youth support in regards to university fees. Once the coalition came to an end, they found themselves taking all the blame for the bad parts of the coalition, whilst their partners took all the credit for the good. The party's then leader, Nick Clegg, took them into the next election, but quickly stood down when his party dropped from 57 seats in parliament to 8, almost eliminating the party from all relevance in the minds of the voters and returning their worst election result since forming in 1988. Clegg, openly Atheist, was then replaced by the evangelical Christian Tim Farron, one of the few Liberal to maintain his seat following the electoral collapse of the party.

Tim Farron had dealt with questions on his religious views throughout his political career, particularly on abortion and LGBT rights where he went against the common opinion of the countries masses, and even further with faith healing, of which supported in a letter to the Advertising Standard Authority who had questioned its benefits. Despite this, plenty of politicians have had successful careers, whilst holding views that fall outside of the mainstream, whether it me Nigel Farage's belief in a 'fifth column' of Islamic Extremists in the UK, or the British National Party's platform to make it illegal to portray homosexuality positively in the media. Each of these politicians believes in their view and outwardly promotes it, choosing to embody it through their actions and behaviours, Farron, instead, either flip flopped or attempted to avoid the question. When asked his opinion on LGBT rights, he questioned why he is being challenged when if he was Jewish or Muslim they wouldn't do so, he then said it wasn't a sin, before later admitting the Liberal Democrat Central Leadership had forced him to answer in that manner. Whereas as the BNP and Farage would happily tell you why they came to the opinion they had, and more than gladly pull up as much evidence as they can muster, regardless of its viability, Farron instead pointed at the church and said 'that's what they told me', shirking off an responsibility for his own beliefs. If you want to hold any sort of belief system, you need to embody it, with religion, you would be better off talking about having a personal conversation with God, than simply saying you were relaying the orders of the church, as it provides evidence to the masses that you are both incapable of critical thinking, not a trait the masses are looking for. 53% of the UK considers itself Christian, yet only 1.15% go to church, so relaying messages they are actively avoiding, is not going to endear them to you, as they have no context on which to base them. Of course, in the UK, 26 Bishops sit in the House of Lords and can therefore impact how you run the government quite significantly, so it's a very important to pay lip service to a religion if need be, and it's a cheap price to pay for that obstacle to be removed and to keep the 53% on side, but that is about as far as you want your religious convictions to take you.

Making friends

No rise to prominence can be properly managed without the creation of an inner circle, a select group of allies and individuals that can be trusted to surround you to legitimise your position and work to expand your influence without seeking any limelight of their own.

These are the world's beta people, social afterthoughts those who have no desire to rise to the top, but retain the need to feed from those who do. Most will naturally move into your circle as you rise up the ladder, but it's important to retain those whose sole goal is to remain in a secondary position, and not to jump you at the last moment. Former UK Prime Minister Tony Blair, in order to support the brand of New Labour, created an inner circle that pushed both him and the new ideas, but fell short with Gordon Brown who craved the top position. Needing him to step aside in the short term to allow him an easier rise to power, Blair promised him the top job once his part of the New Labour project was done. This would later come to bite him and tarnish both their legacies when Brown sought power earlier than Blair intended creating a crisis for the party's leadership.

Inner circles will also help maintain your position when facing internal opposition. As you rise up the ladder, diluting the party's ideology and introducing new ideas, lower status politicians will attack you in order to maintain the status quo they are familiar with. These unskilled politicians will see being counter to your popular vision as a sign of intelligence rather than belligerence, and will fight you in order develop their position within your internal opposition. You won't have time to put out each individual fire as it arises, but a strong inner circle, with its tentacles reaching into each internal political circle, will do this for you, as each attack on your person is an attack on them and their future.

The easiest stock to draw from whilst developing your inner circle is from political ideologues who already support what you intend to do. Tony Blair, Gordon Brown and their counterpart, who would later become Home Secretary, Ed Balls were all members of the Fabian Society, a left-wing forum for political thought. The society sought to advance democratic socialism without the traditional socialist requirement of revolution, instead seeking gradualist change through small indeterminate movements running counter to the Labour party's famous 'Clause IV' which essentially tied the party to both socialism and the nationalisation of key industries. With the help of his inner circle, as well as those seeking an improved relationship with the new leader, he was able to reword Clause IV in a manner that neither tied them to their socialist past, nor anything in particular outside what we would consider a strong rebranding by a skilled politician. The inner circle, and their allies, soon became New Labour. The now belligerent outsiders, Old Labour, were given a nominal roles in cabinet to convince them they still had a say in the running of the party, John Prescott becoming deputy prime minister, but in truth they were as distant from the parties decision making processes as the Conservative party was.

If you can't find similar ideologues, the inner circle is better made up of career politicians rather than those who are in politics in order to improve the lives of their constituents. Career politicians are looking for longevity in their roles, and will follow the leader who they most believe gives them the best chance in securing their income, having few qualifications in other job fields that would reward them with a similar paycheque, Jeffery Archer once comparing a lifer he met in prison, who joked about being unqualified for anything outside the walls, to an MP who had expressed the same concerns when standing for re-election. These politicians are not in short supply: whereas in 1950 a survey carried out by Herbert

Nicholas showed that only 30 of the 1200 candidates running for either the Labour or Tory ticket could be described as a 'political insider' (outnumbered by 39 coal miners and 39 people who had simply inherited wealth), in 2009 a full quarter of all the candidates standing had no work experience outside of politics. These politicians are in no mood for the ideological whims of a leader who could lose them their jobs, houses and the ability to feed their families in a poorly thought-out attempt to better the lives of their countrymen. Instead they feel that they are much better off cosying up to the leader who offers them long-term employment. The quid pro quo for these characters is simple: they will defend your position, as long as you are beneficial to theirs.

As the career politicians you brought into your circle won't hold ideologies of their own, preferring pragmatism over actual plans or ideas, and they will attack anyone who threatens the status quo in order protect their position. Your political enemies – inside your party but outside the inner circle – will be cast as conspiracy theorists by your allies as they fight to maintain their position, as well as to earn brownies points to improve their standing with you, the pay of higher offices beckoning them into our preferred behaviours. Membership of an inner circle is a fleeting role for the careerists, who know a change in leader could banish them to the touchlines of the political game: Sadiq Khan and Rosie Winterton, both worked closely with the New Labour leadership, but are now considered hostile outsiders to the Corbyn section of the Labour party, while Corbyn himself was an outsider to Blair's New Labour. Because of this, your inner circle will seek to eliminate all threats to their position, only getting angrier the closer they are to doom, knowing that the opportunity for them to make real money is coming to an end. They will use both violent rhetoric and sabotage, along with simple lies to keep you in your position, on the understanding it keeps them in theirs.

Because of this it's important to keep politics out of your inner circle. The career politician will look at you, look at what you stand for and then weigh up whether they think your ideas will keep them in work, they are therefore as susceptible to the frames and brands we create as the masses are. A politician who still believes in politics will want to see the plans you've drawn up and ask if that's what's best for society, never a good question for a member of the inner circle to ask should it stoke worries in others. Any problem perceived in a plan they are looking to invest in, may well lead them to leaving your circle and naming you a traitor to the cause, hugely damaging if they are seen as a member of your inner circle by the masses. This fate befell Canadian Prime Minister Stephen Harper who saw his former minister of Veteran Affairs, Eve Adams decrying his policies as hard-line and mean-spirited, something her new leader, Justin Trudeau would use against him on his way toward victory at the next election.

Once you have your inner circle in place, it's time to put them to work.

The qualifications held by career politicians are always able to be broken down into 'has worked in politics', with little to no particular expertise outside of roles they have been given within the party. Although this seems to be to their deficit, as governmental departments tend to require experts in order for them to be run efficiently, this is not the case.

Career politicians can be incredibly effective for you in roles they are seemingly unqualified for thanks to their lack of relatable knowledge. When in charge of a governmental department the career politician's role is to pass on instructions from the central party and to develop their charge in the vision you give them. Any pushback from those lower on the departmental ladder are ignored, regardless of the fact they may well be more qualified than the department's head, as the career politician won't be able to translate their concerns in a manner that they understand or which relates to the central party's political direction – the only cause they believe in. Out of either arrogance or stupidity the career politician will refuse to believe it is they who lacks the ability to make an informed choice, and that the department they run simply doesn't understand what they are trying to achieve or the wider political picture. The career politician will take no advice from insubordinates who simply don't understand the great task ahead of them, sticking to the grand plan that you set forth and trusted them to lead. After the Republican primaries, Ben Carson worked closely with Donald Trump, who he had developed a close friendship with throughout the race and once the election was over, he was rewarded with the position of governmental Secretary of Housing and Urban Development. If he had been tasked with the development of this department, he would have been wholly unqualified for the role. Instead, his role was simply to hand down orders in line with what the central party needed – in this case a $6.5 billion budget cut and the elimination of a community development grant he had strongly supported during his own campaign.

A strong inner circle will also allow you avert some risk. Moving into the political sphere means you are opening up your entire life to public and media scrutiny, so it's important you take the time to look back through your life and take account of anything that may be deemed a risk to your aspirations. This may include immature comments on social media, sexual transgressions, drug use or anything that may offend a sizeable chunk of the electorate. It's equally as important not to mix up your own morality with that of the populace who may well hold higher standards, particularly in a country where there is a strong religious undertone or an active, highly competitive, traditional media or a strong NSM presence.

The seemingly obvious answer is to avoid any illicit actions throughout your life, upholding your civic virtue, but this is not always possible as moral boundaries are always changing. Something seen as acceptable at one point in time is not guaranteed to remain so in the future. Tobacco lobbying during the 1950s and 60s was an accepted part of the political process, yet today it would be a death sentence for a politician to be linked to those lobbyists, and the same is true with any anti-LGBTQ rhetoric. Although a negative attitude towards the LGBTQ community and any advancement of their rights would have been seen as a defence of family values in former times, in today's world it is now seen by the younger generation as a prehistoric attitude, so a balance needs to be found. Aside from the changing moral landscape, its important take into consideration the communities you align yourself with. It is well known that many prominent US politicians were previously members of the Ku Klux Klan, some joining to shore up support for local elections, whilst others held the deeply offensive beliefs of the group, but in either case, none saw membership as being that big of a threat to their political credentials, notably David Duke, a former Grand Wizard who attempted to run for president, and Robert C Byrd a former Klan recruiter who was a Senator for 51 years in West Virginia. Yet in the modern world, simply being a member of a secret society can be dangerous, George W. Bush's association with the Skull and Bones and UK Prime Minister David Cameron's involvement with the Piers Gaveston Society, caused both significant problems. Neither 'secret society' was an actively political group, focusing more on the 'brotherhood' of members, but when your opposition are allowed to make your secrets public it soon becomes open season for conspirators to make up their own theories and start corrupting your brand. It's therefore important to identify these potential risks, as well as any possible sources that may leak information: old friends, angry ex-partners or business associates – a tight inner circle will eliminate most of these risks, but don't make the mistake in believing that any particular person in your life is above betrayal should the timing suit them

The two biggest risks to your political career are any betrayals of trust you've carried out, which tend go hand in hand with being a politician, and anything that disrupts your brand, as those two facets will move voters away from you as they seek to guarantee the short-term rewards they expect from the person they put in charge. In both cases the easiest way of avoiding any fallout from a problem is to simply transfer the risk away from your own person, onto someone else. Donald Trump has always played it fast and loose with the bankruptcy laws, but when his businesses fall into disrepute he can distance himself from the catastrophe by laying the blame at the feet of the board of directors running the company. As they are reliant on the 'Trump' brand to maintain their business, no matter how damaged, they are unlikely to fight back. Furthermore, as it's a group of people assuming the blame they are unlikely to defend themselves. They know that if they do so they risk putting their head above the foxhole, becoming the face linked with the disaster and assuming all the blame, as opposed to sharing the burden with the rest of the board.

Breaches of the public's trust are harder to transfer, but normally a quid pro quo can be found with someone who is willing to take responsibility for an incident in return for a future payoff. The individual will be tied deeply to the plot as any potential reward is reliant on you remaining in your position, so if they accept the deal you can count on their continued loyalty. When Ronald Reagan came under fire during the Iran-Contra affair, where the US was secretly selling arms to Iran despite their own embargo, Oliver North stood up and took responsibility to spare the reigning president's blushes. In return, he got limited immunity for conviction, and then in 1994 the Republican Party supported him as he ran for senate in Virginia. Once that adventure came to an end with electoral defeat, he started working with Republican-allied Fox News, becoming one of their more successful presenters for over 15 years.

If you want to avoid using people in this manner, having them make personal sacrifices in order to protect your own position, there is an early opportunity within your political career to rehabilitate some risks of that you may have singled out from your past (or present), through 'career modelling', where you develop your brand in such a manner that these incidents can be rehabilitated. When you are branding yourself for the election campaign, take the opportunity to pick out a few risks and minimise their damage if they should come out by building them into your brand. A comparative case exists when comparing Bill Clinton and John F Kennedy.

Bill Clinton built himself up as a trustworthy family man, once making the point that by voting for him you'd be getting two presidents for the price of one, due to his marriage to Hillary. He fought George Bush Sr by arguing that his opponent had broken promises – for example, the raising of taxes — whilst also defending himself from accusations of extra-marital affairs, taking Hillary onto '60 Minutes', a CBS news show, to claim they were in a strong marriage. He developed his character as a down-to-earth honest man who you would want as a neighbour. So when his affair with Monica Lewinsky came out, it rocked the nation. Clinton first started with denials, before eventually admitting to an 'improper relationship', but not before he lied under oath whilst testifying during the Paula Jones trial, which would lead to his impeachment. The fallout of the affair greatly affected not only Al Gore's 2000 campaign, who ran it too cautiously so as not to scare off voters, but Hillary Clinton's 2017 campaign where it was used as a weapon to attack her personally by her opponents.

Yet if we compare Bill Clinton's political career to that of John F Kennedy, a man famous for his many affairs whilst married, a different narrative is presented. He was said to have been involved, at separate times, with Gunilla von Post, Judith Campbell, Mimi Alford and, most famously, Marilyn Monroe, amongst others. During his political career he was seen as a young go-getter and cultivated a relationship with the press to ensure they would treat any controversy in an appropriate manner. The population saw him as a symbol of the new generation, allowing him to write off transgressions as merely lapses as he was coming of age. Whilst many of his contemporaries wrote him off as a playboy, reckless and impatient, the population saw this but forgave it, and because of that, when rumours of further affairs hit the presses, the population were willing to forgive and forget. Even now he gets remembered as one of the United States' most popular presidents, despite having a less than average reign.

What you want to avoid, if at all possible, is bringing someone into the fold with the intention of simply seeking to control them or their message, the hope being that they will be so immensely grateful for your support that they'll change their perception of you and your ideas. You should certainly avoid bringing someone in to silence them, as all you are doing is giving them a platform where they can attack you from an insider position, giving additional weight to their opinions.

Prior to becoming Donald Trump's press secretary, Sean Spicer had worked in public affairs for the Navy reserve, been a communications director for the House Government Reform Committee as well as holding a positions of esteem in a variety of Republican National Committee groups. He was, and remains, immensely qualified for the role, but Spicer had been openly critical of Trump in the past, attacking his statements on illegal immigrants and defending John McCain from the attack on his war record. Still, Trump persisted with bringing him into the fold, in the hope that by controlling the man, he could silence him, as well as perhaps offering a sense of outreach to other anti-Trump Republican politicians who felt alienated by the rise of his presidency.

Instead, what he actually managed to do was to demote a rival and force him to be the spokesperson, giving him a platform to directly damage the president. Most observers would be hard pressed to believe that Spicer truly backed the administration: his press conferences were messy and his distance from Trump led to him taking each attack on the presidency as a personal attack on himself, as he didn't have the answers the media we're looking for. Trump committed the same sin with Chris Christie, bringing a former rival into the inner circle, then seemingly working to disparage him at every turn. This form of score settling doesn't reap rewards, it only serves to cast questions on the control you have on your own party. Spicer has made Trump look like he has a weak inner circle, whilst his actions with Christie have cast him as a bully pushing moderate Republicans away, the stories that have leaked since that point have only further strengthened the opinion that the Trump presidency has little control over his inner circle, let alone the wider party.

Inviting a potential enemy into the fold will always open you up to a lot of potential problems. Instead, allow them a platform outside of the inner circle where distance renders their attacks mute. Outside of the circle, the opposition are weak and easy to frame as outsiders who aren't allowed to participate in the real political conversations as they are not qualified enough to do so. It's an easy attack to make as the masses will see an exiled politician kicking up a fuss for the sake of attention. George Galloway fought stringently against New Labour and the Iraq War, but with little comeback from anyone in a real position of power: Tony Blair, in response to Galloway's call for the troops in Iraq to ignore 'illegal orders', was simply 'His comments were disgraceful and wrong. The National Executive will deal with it', distancing himself from the man even whilst offering a solution to the problem. As an exiled outsider, Galloway worked wonders for the New Labour administration. Not only did people think he was nutty, but if any additional politician had thoughts about attacking the inner circle, they were now able to see the consequences: expulsion from the party, a reputation in tatters, and eventually an appearance on the TV show, Celebrity Big Brother.

Of all the members of your inner circle, the role of your number two is the one to get right. not only are they the first opportunity you will have to impress the masses with your decision making prowess, of all the people close to you they are the most likely to harbour higher aspirations, as they will assume that their position as number 2 acts as qualification enough for the top job. Therefore, as with all political decisions, there are tactical considerations you must make when handing out the role, in particular when it comes to balancing out your offer.

If you are young, it is important to pick an experienced number two that will help convince your internal supporters that there is a calming voice and a safety net to help reduce the impact from any immature whims you may have, or talk you out of any sporadic action that may impact the party's future.

Obama was a two term governor, and although he was a clear favourite to win, he chose Joe Biden as his number two, who represented an 18 year age gap, over his other option of the similarly aged Evan Bayh, which would have presented them as the 'youth' ticket. The benefit in Biden was not, however, in his age, but his experience in the workings of government that his counterparts lacked. Since first being elected in 1972, he had chaired the Senate Judiciary Committee, the Foreign Relations Committee and the International Narcotics Committee, things that the voter may not pay much attention to, but professional politicians did. Those experiences were required for the Democrat National Committee to confidently back any potential president, let alone a rookie, so Obama, knowing he didn't possess those skills, imported them and strengthened his position. However, if Obama moved to get an older running mate to shore up his own experience and relax his internal detractors, McCain instead saw the age of Obama as a pivot point in itself, one that may drive young voters away from him, and into his opponents awaiting arms.

McCain sought to counter this by bringing in Sarah Palin, a running mate 28 years his junior, who had served as the ninth governor of Alaska and was one of the darlings of the Republican Party. If McCain was hoping to add some youthful exuberance to his ticket he was mistaken, whereas Obama's age could be correlated to his idealism, Palin showed herself to be another ultra-conservative, a group McCain was already appealing to, with far right ideas on abortion, same-sex marriage, and climate change. Whilst Obama could be seen as the future of the Democrat party and its potential, the presence of Biden simply shoring up the traditional Democrat offer for those that may have been nervous voting for an unexperienced leader, Palin simply repeated what McCain was already selling, attracting no new supporters.

Strangely, though they ignored this strategy, the expansion of the 'political offer' was not a new tactic for McCain's party, and was used by outgoing Republican President, George W. Bush during his earlier races for governor in Texas, arguing that he could, and would, work with both Democrat and Republican officials to offer middle ground Democrat supporters a guilt-free vote, expanding his appeal and winning him the role. Moves like this signal to the masses you can compromise and that they won't be cut out of any benefits that are received if they vote for you, tempting supporters to cross party lines if your opponent makes a mistake or if they are looking for a guilt-free vote should they support one of your harder policies. You may be reducing taxes by cutting social welfare, or banning immigrants, and opposition supporters may want to vote for these policies but can't convince themselves to cross the party lines. Signalling that you will work with your opponents, gives them the excuse that they aren't voting for a real enemy. McCain did have the option of bringing in Democrat Joe Liebermann as his running mate but rejected the idea for fear of losing the Republican centre he ended up doubling down on. Hilary Clinton would later make the same mistake, deciding to run with Tim Kaine, on the basis he could speak Spanish, as opposed bringing former adversary Bernie Saunders into the fold who offered a wider level of appeal.

Your second should work to expand your offer, offering the masses the potential of change whilst you secure your own support, but keep you choices in the context of the career politicians. The number 2 position should be the highest level your chosen politician is likely to attain, whether it be through lack of charisma, secrets you hold on them, or lack of internal support within the wider party, however, there are alternative uses for the number two spot.

The ability to highlight and remove people you perceive as a threat to your position is an incredibly useful skill to have as a politician. Not all enemies will be holding pitchforks at your door, most will masquerade as allies waiting for a time to strike, whilst others may exist in the background, pulling strings with their political allies as they seek to manoeuvre themselves into an advantageous place. After demoting Geoffrey Howe out of the foreign office, only awarding him the role in the first place after removing him as Home Secretary, Margret Thatcher brought the title of Deputy Prime Minister out of its 26 year retirement to bestow upon on him as an act of appeasement. Although considered a potential successor to Thatcher, with their cold relationship it was clear to the Prime Minister that a disgruntled Howe offered more problems to her leadership than solutions, so by handing him a symbolic role she blunted any attack he could use, as an attack on her leadership would also be an attack on his inability to change anything as her 'number two'. Her successor as Prime Minister (who incidentally also succeeded Howe into the foreign office) John Major also used the Deputy Prime Minister role for the same reason. Facing leadership challenge after leadership challenge, Major found his enemies were starting to rally around Michael Heseltine, despite his challenger having no real desires to lead the party. Major pulled him into a two hour meeting prior to the leadership vote, then announced him as the Deputy Prime Minister. With Heseltine's allies losing their chosen leader, and no one else willing or able to stand up for leadership at short notice left them rudderless, taking Heseltine's appointment as a small victory in itself, they voted to keep Major in power, hoping their man would influence Major in the right way.

Creating enemies and exiling the unneeded from your political inner circle, can unfortunately also cause problems. There is always the chance that something you identified as a risk could evolve into a crisis when an alienated, or insulted, third party seizes upon it and makes it public knowledge in an attempt to end your political aspirations. There are three elements to any political crisis:

1.   It presents a threat to your brand

2.   It revealed itself with short or no prior notice

3.   There is a short window for a decision to be made

Being attacked on all sides with people now questioning your ability to lead, your actions need to be immediate in case you lose the confidence of the public as well as your inner circle. By its nature a crisis will change your landscape so you won't be able to maintain any systems that you have built to control your public relations. You won't be able to rely on middle-men or any medium you have previously used, as the masses will expect a change to occur in your behaviour to match their shock. This is a mistake many politicians and celebrities have committed: when confronted with a crisis they may make an appearance on a TV show or media outlet that they have featured on in the past in order to offer a scripted apology and bat away easy questions. This only serves to convince the masses you are trying to control your surroundings to protect yourself and ignore the problem. Another mistake politicians make is to try to maintain their brand by apologising or trying to shift the blame to an unwilling partner, when the masses have already chosen who they want to hang. This is one of the few times it is acceptable to let your brand slip and reveal a more personal side of yourself so that the masses know you are taking everything seriously.

The only successful way of dealing with a crisis is to move the conversation straight into the solution stage, taking the frame away from 'what happened' – generally controlled by external sources, such as the media – towards 'what's being done', where you can control the conversation. In this time, don't focus on your own personal standing, but instead on coming up with the plan that will lead to a solution. Every crisis is an opportunity to build yourself up in the eyes of the masses as a 'fixer', plus it removes your person from the centre of the conversation. The plan should be on the table as soon as possible, but you don't need a media source holding you to targets that you set in the heat of the moment. Instead, you must decide what success is when you achieve it, declaring mission accomplished only when you can offer the masses a quantifiable goal, and when any more energy spent on the problem no longer returns similar rewards, retreat silently from the problem. Only make vague promises at the start, such as 'creating a better future' or 'improving the lives of those affected', by not setting a quantifiable target, you can't be held to one releasing you from your obligations to the community.

For their part, members of the inner circle are not perfect and will sometimes put themselves into situations that are disruptive to your political career. In this case, distance yourself from the person and immediately fire them before cutting ties. Don't waste energy trying to defend them, as all you'll do is shift blame that should be their sole property onto yourself, as the masses start to relate you to one another. If they hold any position within your party, replace them in the short term with someone who is popular and trustworthy in the eyes of the public, rather than qualified for the role, to start rebuilding trust. Ensure the former ally is not able to maintain any position of responsibility: if they want to go to rehab, for example, ensure the rhetoric is that you sent them to rehab, rather than that they volunteered, allowing the masses to see you as the one in control. As soon as time allows, move on from the ally. The political ladder will allow them time to recover and rebuild their political career over time, but you don't want to be forever linked to a disgraced politician simply because they were once part of your inner circle.

In the event of a crisis the trick is to take control of the conversation, and, in the words of Lanny Davies, 'Tell it early, tell it all, tell it yourself'. By allowing others to take the conversation and frame it in a manner that suits their own ends, it will be difficult to protect yourself. You are the source of information, so ensure that you are the one telling it to the media, not any whistle-blowers or people trying to carve out their own paths through you. Make sure the information you hand out is understandable to the masses by avoiding complicated terms – opponents will be working hard to muddle your words and look for inconsistencies to confuse your message and paint you as untrustworthy. If there is an opportunity to blame a third party, be wary you are not coming off as petty, and make sure that you personally don't attribute blame. You can sack someone by saying they are 'unsuited to the role in the present circumstances'; you aren't sending someone to rehab to battle their addictions, you are 'getting them help so they can return to being the person their friends and family love'.

Also don't be afraid of these crises, they can be a good thing. Politicians who recover from them will see a huge increase in popularity as they legitimise themselves in the eyes of the public as a go-getter and a solution finder. It's a good opportunity to show your character and commitment to the country, so don't see a crisis as something that limits your leadership or potential. In fact, many leaders actively seek out crises to help bolster their support: it's why politicians like war so much. Thatcher's government saw their approval jump through the roof during the Falkands War, whilst George W. Bush saw his approval peak during the invasion of Iraq.

With all crises, the trick is ensuring that you are quick to the table with a solution. Centralise control and make sure there is only a single source that people can go to for information, involving only trusted allies. Be ready to purge anyone from your inner circle if they are damaging your brand,

and make sure you are the person who is credited with finding a solution.

The Future of Politics

Despite the pressures of the information and technological revolutions sweeping the planet, the world has remained relatively straightforward for the politician.

The social changes brought on through the rise of the Internet have left the Western Governmental systems relatively unscathed, despite the fact that many of the stakeholders who hold positions of power within the said systems maintain beliefs that run counter to the social and political desires of the now incredibly active New Social Movements. Liberal Democracy, with its focus on the individual, is still held up as being the perfect system of government by these self-proclaimed revolutionaries trying to overthrow the political hegemony but more and more they seem to be moving away from traditional political participation and instead trying to operate on their own plain, only engaging with the democratic game when absolutely necessary, for example, trying to get a particular politician out of office or pushing a very specific agenda.

By operating separately from the traditional political game, NSM's offer no real solutions to their perceived problems outside their empty rhetoric; they don't seek to promote their own leaders into political office, seeing policy-led agendas a betrayal to the wider cause, and yet will still defend the institution of democracy from any attack, seeing it as the last bastion of freedom, despite their own lack of engagement. Their behaviours are understandable as a reaction to the collapse in trust they have had with us, but the contradiction of defending the status quo of the democratic institution and refusing to partake, serves to allow us the monopoly of power within the state, and a reduced amount of contenders for our position, making it a very comfortable existence for the pragmatic politician. These circumstances, along with the collapse of ideology as a means of control, have released us from our bonds of public service, and no longer needing to be subservient to anyone else's beliefs we are free to chase our own ends and protect our own interests. The only real threats to our position are now other politicians, who operate under the same rule book we do, and dealing with them is why this guide exists.

The world the politician fights their battles in today is a very different arena to those of the past. The era of narrative-led news, internet-based social movements and the death of the two big ideologies has led to a brave new world where the masses are looking for easy answers to relieve them of the stress of a constant barrage of information. At their heart, however, they haven't changed in their desires: we know at their base level they are still after improvement of their own lot, and will take smaller guaranteed returns over large, yet distant, promises. Because of this we need to remain clear and concise in what we are offering, and aim it at as large a part of the population as possible, using terms that can be interpreted in a number of ways and applied to a number of different situations. It's also important to remind the masses of the urgency required of them in throwing their support behind you. Any delay could be catastrophic for their future, so they need to be loud and proud whilst holding up your banner. From this, we can do away with the myth that the best politician is the one who designs the best argument; instead focus on cultivating the most urgent frame, the strongest brand and the most subservient team.

The brand is the first focus, as you don't want to be left behind and ignored simply because you don't fit with your audience's perception, or appeal to a small demographic who hold no real political sway, such as the poverty stricken. Instead we want to build a brand that people can get behind and relate to on a level that they too believe they are part of. This allows for us to short-circuit the trust issues that unfairly surround politicians by asking that they don't trust in us, but in themselves – after all, they would never believe it would be possible for them to pick bad friends. A strong brand will have the masses judge your actions by their own intentions, as opposed to our intended consequences, allowing us to act pragmatically, and further increasing the freedom allowed to us following the death of ideology. The absence of this particular political force has been beneficial for both us and the masses. Ideology forced politicians into actions not of their making, handing out plans from on high for the sake of a wider vision that might never come to fruition. Instead, by focusing on a brand, we can design our own future, even being able to rehabilitate policies that were previously rejected by the masses by simply rewording their prose.

The brand also has the benefit of creating a strong yet flexible foundation which attracts sycophantic and career politicians who are simply looking to secure their own positions, without reaching for any time in the sun themselves. Believing you to be the harbinger of their future, they will be your tentacles as you reach down to exert control through every part of your political party, allowing you to move freely in the wider political world. Enemies will always spring up, but with a strong enough inner circle you should be able to cast them aside and castrate them as 'wacko' outsiders that the masses should ignore. These career politicians will also support any frame you put forward for an election, knowing that your success is their success, regardless of how nervous the plan may actually make them feel. Without their own brands, allies or successful track record, they know that stepping out of line will see them labelled a traitor, and with no incentive for others to join them they will slip into obscurity not long before unemployment – the career politician's nightmare.

Nonetheless, the frame remains key. The narrative-led 24-hour news cycle and the rise of social media have vastly shortened the attention spans of the masses who are hit by a daily avalanche of information that would exhaust them to sort through. Instead, a frame gives us the ability to draw their focus onto a particular set of topic where we are strongest, and build an entire election around that. By partaking in policy extremism, over-stating solutions and refusing to discuss any other frame that another politician is trying to promote, we can take control of the political conversation and, therefore, take the votes. Other politicians will attempt the same thing, but believing it's possible to obtain 100% of the vote they are easy to cast aside as they try to please everyone and not commit to anything.

The information and technological revolutions of the 21st century have changed our world considerably. The increased interconnectivity of society has allowed new movements to arise, as well as helping social scientists to work to greatly increase our knowledge of what we are as a species. This, mixed with western society's focus on liberalism and personal freedom, has allowed individuals such as Bill Gates, Elon Musk and Richard Branson to inspire innovation and creativity in the masses not seen before, meaning the world could have become a much more dangerous place for politicians. Instead, the belief that there exists no middle ground between liberal democracy and communist dictatorship has protected our position: we are now only required to portray behavioural changes in order to create the illusion of trust to match the whims of a clustered society to protect ourselves and maintain the status quo. And this is important: society benefits from the strong foundations led by conservatism and tradition; the ideas perpetrated by the NSMs could be dangerous, but instead the masses are happy to allow the continuation of the liberal democratic management system, purely out of fear of the unknown. This attitude, helpfully, secures our position in society as the upper management, being the only ones qualified to run the political infrastructure.

After all, the masses aren't going to vote for themselves.

www.ingramcontent.com/pod-product-compliance
Lightning Source LLC
Chambersburg PA
CBHW020304290526
45784CB00003B/1354